MW01285045

THE GENIUS WAY ®

Expressing Your Unique Gifts:

A Ten-Step Path to Life Fulfillment

BEN HUMMELL LPC, LMFT

THE GENIUS *WAY*®
Expressing Your Unique Gifts
A Ten-Step Path to Life Fulfillment
Copyright 2022 © Ben Hummell

Published by
Genius Publishing
Ashland, Oregon
www.benhummell.com

All rights reserved. No part of this book may be reproduced in any form or by any electronic or mechanical means, including information storage and retrieval systems, without written permission from the author, except in the case of a reviewer, who may quote brief passages embodied in critical articles or in a review.

Trademarked names appear throughout this book. Rather than use a trademark symbol with every occurrence of a trademarked name, names are used in an editorial fashion, with no intention of infringement of the respective owner's trademark.

The information in this book is distributed on an "as is" basis, without warranty. Although every precaution has been taken in the preparation of this work, neither the author nor the publisher shall have any liability to any person or entity with respect to any loss or damage caused or alleged to be caused directly or indirectly by the information contained in this book.

Cover design by Nikitas Kavouklēs
Interior layout by Veronica Yager, YellowStudios

ISBN: 978-0-9971616-1-8
Library of Congress Control Number: 2021924570

To Yang, Henry, and Cici
with love and gratitude.

CONTENTS

PREFACE

"Think of the fierce energy concentrated in an acorn. You bury it into the ground, and it explodes into an oak."
—George Bernard Shaw

THE UNASSUMING ACORN HAS long been an archetypal symbol of something very small that mysteriously contains the potential to grow and transform into something much grander, more enduring, and more complex.

The image of the acorn holds an ancient allusion to a promise, a journey, and a destiny.

It is truly difficult to look at an acorn without a sense of awe when you realize that every oak that has ever spread its roots to soak up water, and grown branches and leaves to reach for the sun, was once contained in such a tiny seed as little more than DNA, possibility, and potential.

An acorn appears ubiquitous and insignificant, but it embodies all it needs to expand into a singularly different presence: physical, self-efficacious, unapologetic, and with the requisite audacity to exist as more than what it already is.

But why stop with the acorn? Every seed is a holder of this archetype and wondrous function, each one pregnant with the particular qualities imbued within it. The "fierce energy" from Shaw's quote is the miracle that takes place in everything that grows from a seed, springing forth from its unexpressed potential to develop into something quite unexpectedly different and unique.

We can look through a scientific lens at the mechanics of how an acorn grows into an oak tree and come away with an intellectual understanding of its biological processes. But a deeper way to regard its "fierce energy" isn't with science or mathematics, or by measurements and standards, but by bearing witness to the profound mystery of its very existence. We need to employ a lens that is less corporeal—a lens that is something like poetry or faith. Or like art, feeling, or love.

And so it is with the potential for self-expression contained in each one of us. Science can explain how our bodies and brains work, but no scientific tools can uncover or measure what makes our lives valuable, meaningful, or deep. That specific task and understanding is an inside job. It's up to each one of us to discover that potential for ourselves, using our inner senses as a guide.

Between the hard edges of science and the subtle world of mystery, there is a liminal realm where psychology, philosophy, and spirituality reign. Somewhere within this realm is a way to approach a sense of the innate energy that drives the journey of all living things toward their complete unfoldment. And although there is no equation or instrument that can measure this energetic drive, we can learn to see and feel it as an aspect of our lives. We can give it a name to help us recognize and care for it as the gift that it is.

The "fierce energy" of the acorn is what I call the *Genius Drive* in humans. It's the equivalent storehouse of energy, potential, interest, and creativity of expression on an individual human level that can be uncovered, expressed, and lived. It's what can enable each person to move throughout their life with a sense of direction and purpose.

This isn't a book about learning how to "cash in" on your hidden Genius talents to become rich and successful.

There are enough books about that.

The Genius Way is a process of learning how to recognize the potential expression in your individual Genius seed and how to use it as your internal compass for identity, life direction, guidance, and self-expression throughout the whole of this one precious life.

INTRODUCTION

I HAVE ALWAYS FOUND my fellow human beings innately fascinating, especially as I am getting to know them more deeply and quietly, listening to how they've framed their life stories, and learning what they hope and dream for in their future. Along the way, I developed a knack for seeing the psychology of a person as distinctly separate from the existential spark at their core that makes them singularly precious and unique.

Throughout my psychotherapy career, a consistent issue that I've heard clients report in addition to their initial complaint is a general feeling of purposelessness. They describe feeling stuck in habitual patterns or psychological ruts, not knowing how to get out of them, or not knowing what to do to create forward movement in their life. Often, even after the primary symptoms that brought them to therapy are treated and their normal functioning is restored, the issue of life direction and purposeful forward life movement remains unaddressed.

A question I began to wrestle with was this: Why is the specific issue of finding life direction consistently resistant to longstanding and proven psychological interventions?

In the practice of therapy, the life direction issue is almost always left unexplored or unresolved because it feels too broad or vague, or it doesn't rank on the top ten list of "real problems." It can even seem like an indulgence or a luxury to name it as one. Many clients, particularly those whose outward lives are functioning well in terms of their basic needs, even feel a sense of shame in bringing it up. Dissatisfaction with life direction hasn't been identified in the Diagnostic and Statistical Manual of Mental Disorders (the DSM-V), and insurance companies won't pay professionals to treat or address it.

What I've realized is that the life direction issue doesn't get addressed or resolved by psychological intervention simply because it's not actually a problem in the first place.

Wait . . . what?

Let me explain.

Instead of seeing life direction as a problem in the traditional sense, I have come to understand the issue of life direction as a transpersonal circumstance or situation. It is present in all of us in some form and at some time in our life. Identifying and refining our life direction and purpose is actually a uniquely human developmental phenomenon and task.

The struggle with finding life direction feels like an individual problem because most of us in modern times haven't been given any instruction or frame of reference about what it feels like to be called upon by existence to grow into a deeper and fuller expression of ourselves. To address this with my clients, I began to work with them on their life direction issue not as a psychological problem to be healed, but as an existential task that they are being called to enter into and complete.

Working within a person's psychology means working primarily with what has been wounded in them and is in need of healing, while working with the existential core of a person is to work with their seed of identity or their *Genius* that simply needs a channel or avenue of expression. To address the existential issue separately from the psychological one, I needed a name and framework to set them apart.

I developed **The Genius Way** as a path for addressing our existential calling to find our life direction.

The nature of our individual Genius is to express something (or some things) *in particular*. This need is essential: it is of our essence. It is primal, in that we are born with it, and is therefore deeper than our psychology. Ignoring or suppressing it doesn't make it go away, because it is a human issue, built into the human experience. Whether we believe it or not, something in us has a need for life direction with a personal sense of meaning and purpose. And it's up to each one of us to figure this out for ourself.

Life direction isn't just about which career to choose, where to live, or whom to marry. It is more foundational than that. To address it, we first have to acknowledge that we have been born with a Genius that functions to carry and express our inner gifts, talents, callings, and purpose. That's *its* job. It knows how to do it. *Our* job as individuals is to identify our Genius qualities and give them a seat at the table of our identity, along with the identity we've built from our psychological development and life experiences. And we can do this simply by the daily acknowledgment of our Genius, a commitment to creating an avenue of expression for it, and by finding a way to practice our Genius expressions.

THE PROBLEM OF PURPOSELESSNESS

When our Genius self isn't allowed an avenue of expression, we can certainly feel it. Our unexpressed potential shows up in our emotional field as a sense of purposelessness. The feeling of being stuck or stagnant is often a message that our Genius wants us to move. And although the feeling of purposelessness may appear in a list of depressive symptoms, the sense of purposelessness that comes from not expressing our Genius potential feels markedly different.

That's because somewhere in our individual awareness, we know that we have an existential task to complete, namely becoming a fuller expression of our original Genius self, and that we're not currently doing the work. So bear with me here when I say that feeling this way is actually a good thing. To feel uncomfortable about being stuck or a vague inner prodding to shift something in our life shows us that stagnation isn't our natural state.

The seed of expression that we hold in our Genius is meant to grow and develop throughout the entirety of our lives. But since we have not been given a frame of reference in which to place this perpetual feeling of purposelessness, we suffer individually with the shame or confusion of not knowing how to be the best version of ourselves, and the feeling that somehow, we *should* know. We haven't been taught that the simple practice of giving our Genius a way to express itself will positively affect the course of our life direction and sense of purpose.

Having no clear life direction means living every day in a state of uncertainty about whether we're making the best decisions, whether we're on the right track, or how to choose a direction for our personal or professional paths.

The Genius Way philosophy holds that to have purposeful life direction, we have to be aligned with our Genius. That is to say, we have to find our Genius, uncover it, and learn to listen to how it communicates with us. In it, we already possess a set of qualities and circumstances *in potentia* that will help us to bring out the best of who we are. In other words, our Genius already knows what it wants to express. We just haven't been taught how to recognize and listen to what it is saying.

A significant part of my work as a psychotherapist and life coach is about listening to what my clients are expressing without words. I notice and listen to body language, facial expressions and affect, pauses in speech, avoidances, hidden interests, and themes. Essentially, what I've learned is that all of us are consistently expressing ourselves via micro-expressions and non-verbal communications that can be seen and listened to for information about our current state of being.

On the life direction and purpose level, we are also consistently expressing ourselves via a meta- or macro-expression. We are actually *saying* something with our life as a whole. I refer to this macro-expression simply as our current *life expression.*

Working with clients to identify their current life expression, I have identified and named two primary **expression drives**, or nexuses of expressive energy from which we act or express ourselves at any given time: the **Wound Drive** and the **Genius Drive**. Depending on which drive is motivating our actions, our life expression is either about *healing* or *creating*. We'll discuss this later in the book.

For now, it is important to be aware of the fact that we are consistently, but mostly *unconsciously*, expressing who we are, and that for our life expression to feel purposeful, it needs to be made consciously and deliberately. With some self-inquiry into what drives our life expression and actions, we can begin to practice a conscious life expression, which aligns us with our inborn Genius and generates feelings of individual life purpose and meaning.

Unless we become aware of the Genius within us and learn to express ourselves from it, we're basing how we live our lives on incomplete information about who we are. It's like not knowing our family heritage or having amnesia about our formative experiences. Not knowing our Genius also deprives us of our access to the self-awareness—and thus the wisdom—we gain from our life choices. Conversely, to uncover our Genius qualities and self is to move through life with direction and purpose.

The Genius Way philosophy holds that each of us has a core fund of identity that is unique to us as individuals, and that it is our job to uncover, explore, and express this core identity during our lifetime. This process actually facilitates life purpose and meaning. It gives us a foundation upon which to build a truly one-of-a-kind life that benefits the world around us.

The importance of learning about our individual Genius goes to the core of what it is to be a fuller and more conscious human being—that is, to be someone who has explored their inner depths, not just for what is in their unconscious, but for what is in their ***primaconscious***, or the part of human consciousness that is the repository of our Genius qualities. (You'll learn about the primaconscious in a later chapter.) Another way of saying this is that a conscious human being hasn't only explored the shadowy world of their wounds and fears, but also the realm of their existential inheritance or their Genius that makes them unique, valuable, and important to the world into which they were born.

I believe that as human beings we need encouragement, inspiration, and validation to become the best of ourselves. This stretching forth or consistent movement in the direction of growth is a natural quality that needs to be nurtured by those of us who understand this function. Like watering a seed, or planting it in an opportune spot to grow, inspiration and encouragement are as essential to humans as water and light are to seeds.

It is in this spirit of encouragement that I offer **The Genius Way** process and philosophy.

THE GENIUS WAY PHILOSOPHY

TO WALK THE PATH of a life direction that emanates from our individual Genius, we have to consciously cultivate our connection to it. Many of us live without a day-to-day awareness of our connection to the creative expression of existence that lives inside us, even though it consistently calls to us to express it. When we make the conscious effort to express this innate aspect of ourselves, we are aligning ourselves with something natural and in flow. We begin to see and feel that existence wants us to express this hidden aspect, and that there is a place for us in this world as our Genius selves. We are actually meant to be here and express our inborn gifts and qualities.

THE CONCEPT OF GENIUS

Let's consider a primary question before we go on: what exactly is Genius? Many people use this word to describe rare individuals who display an uncanny talent in a certain area that gives them an advantage over others—Mozart for music, for example, or Einstein for physics. What I'm referring to as Genius is quite different, so for the journey of this book, I'm asking readers to suspend this common definition of Genius and be open to a different interpretation of the word and the concept.

In my book SUMMONING GENIUS (2016), I give a brief history of the meaning of the term Genius and where the idea comes from. Let's begin with a lightly edited excerpt from that book:

> In modern times, namely the last 100 years or so, the term Genius has been associated with the I.Q., or intelligence quotient, of a person, which is the score someone gets on a standardized test originally developed by French psychologist Alfred Binet. He

1

designed the test [in 1905] to predict how successfully any given student would perform in school. More recent and contemporary versions of this test propose that if someone scores above 140, they fall into the genius range of intelligence, when compared to others who don't score as highly on the same test. Geniuses are considered to be more gifted or special than others, distancing them from the lower-IQ'ed masses.

Back in history, though, the word Genius had a different meaning. Stemming from the Latin words *gignere* (to beget or produce) and *gigno* (the superior or divine nature in everything), a person's Genius was defined as a guiding spirit that accompanies the soul when each person is born. Everyone has one. This spirit is imbued with specific talents, attributes, and creative leanings that make it unique, and therefore precious and intrinsically valuable. All of these specific and unique qualities are seen as gifts that are brought to share with the world.

Each Genius is actually a Genius seed, containing all of the attributes of the mature plant in potential. Given the right circumstances, the seed can grow into its full expression, bearing the fruits and fragrances that it is meant to give outwardly to the world as gifts. The task of all of us human beings, then, is to allow our Genius to integrate into our everyday lives so these gifts can be given, resulting in a felt sense of fulfillment for each of us.

Genius is also seen as a guardian spirit or angel. But the traditional concept of a guardian angel evokes images of our physical protection against evil or dangerous circumstances, whereas Genius's role in our lives is to bear responsibility for keeping our uniqueness alive; it protects our innate qualities, talents, and gifts from becoming lost or diluted. It serves us by reminding us in various ways, and throughout the entirety of our lives, of our personal life callings and the things we were meant to do that will instill individual meaning and purpose. It provides us with both physical and psychological symptoms as indicators of how and when we are ignoring this essential part of ourselves, and where to look for and allow our Genius expression to emerge and manifest. From the time of our birth until our physical death, it continues to care for us, keeping the fire of our creative potential alive by sheltering its flame against the elements of forgetfulness, opposition, and discouragement.

Genius's protection thus extends to the depths of the inner blueprints of our life that were provided to us when we were born. Genius holds us to the universal mandate we are each given to discover and express what those blueprints hold. Some divine architect has made a unique set of these plans for each of us, and the construction and expression of it can be carried out only by the individual who holds them in his or her existential marrow. Our genius knows this and, through a myriad of inner and outer experiences, consistently reminds us of what we individually came here to do.

Throughout this book, I sometimes refer to Genius as the Genius spirit, or our innate Genius, our guardian spirit, or simply Genius. You may want to take notice of how many times the word Genius will trigger a mental connotation of the contemporary "I.Q." definition and observe any accompanying feelings that may arise, ranging from the self-doubt that you even have Genius qualities, to feelings of superiority from singling yourself out as special because of your Genius traits. Remember that these qualities are unique in each of us; every human being who ever was and ever will be born has their own. Most things in the world are identified as being special or precious because of their rarity and limited quantity. So it is with our individual Genius. It expresses a particular flavor only once, and that is through a particular one of us, as we are and as we grow and live. There is absolutely no need to compare or compete with anyone regarding Genius, because living our Genius has at its root a singular historical opportunity for expression. We each carry within us our own unique, precious Genius.

Okay. So far, so good. This encapsulation covers the extent of what most of us understand about the concept of Genius in general. Now let's take it a step further and look at how we can personalize this concept in our daily lives.

ANOTHER WAY TO THINK ABOUT GENIUS

While the Roman idea of Genius attributed our unique individual callings and gifts to a guardian spirit that stayed with us from birth until death, another way of thinking about our embodied Genius is to see our Genius qualities as a kind of existential DNA that is part of who we are individually and that can't be separated from us.

As I have found with my own Genius process and with that of the students and clients I have worked with, grasping the concept of Genius can be inspiring to be sure, but falls short in that the concept of Genius alone doesn't show how us how to locate and express our own Genius qualities. If we hold the idea that each person possesses their individual Genius DNA as foundational, we need to take the next logical step and identify a practical way of actually accessing our Genius.

The Genius Way process addresses this very issue. It is designed to provide a way for you to make your Genius part of your everyday life. It is a journey into self; an education and an expedition into the inner world where your Genius is ready to guide your life path. It is a step-by-step process of listening for, locating, and giving expression to your Genius callings and creating a Genius-based life.

The basic philosophy is simple:

- **Each one of us is born with a set of qualities, skills, and talents that we are meant to spend our lives uncovering and expressing.**

- **There is an actual part of us that is a repository of our Genius qualities (our primaconscious), and we can find this part, open it up, and express it as a foundational aspect of ourselves.**

- **Expressing these inborn talents is the key to living a life with a purposeful direction and a sense of personal meaning and fulfillment.**

FOUNDATIONAL CONCEPTS
OF THE GENIUS WAY

BEFORE WE BEGIN TO work with the process, let's lay out the foundational concepts of the Genius Way. Keep in mind that it's not necessary that you embrace these concepts yourself; just that you have an understanding of the basic language and assumptions we'll be using to go on this journey together.

1. **There is a creative force that has a need to continually express itself as every aspect of existence, humans being one of its expressions.**

The macrocosm, or all of manifest existence, is an expression of a creative force that has a seemingly unstoppable need to express itself. This creative force continuously throws a myriad of expressions out into the physical universe in an attempt to fulfill this need. This creative force is expressing the entire universe out of itself and is learning more and more with each new expression. Each galaxy, planet, human, animal, flower, and stone is an expression of this creative force, and each holds an equal amount of intrinsic value because of its existential origin.

2. **This creative force has passed along this need to self-express to humans, like a genetic trait.**

The microcosm of an individual's need to know and express who they are is the same need that this creative force has to know itself. I want to be very clear here: it is the *exact same need*, as it is the continuation of this creative force's need. It isn't similar, or a version of it, *it is the same need*. What we as individuals are feeling in our need to know and express ourselves has been passed down to us—imbued in us—by this creative force's drive to know and express itself. This is our connection to existence itself and to the other expressions in the universe. To feel this drive personally and choose to make it an important force in how we live our lives is to be connected to the flow of the universe in a personal way.

To honor and continue this expression in and with ourselves is to understand and accept the task given to us as individuals by existence.

Conversely, and as is the case in too many lives, not paying attention to the callings of this inherited Genius Drive, and to live disconnected from its origin, means living and expressing without our inborn sense of direction, purpose, or meaning. Most of us know what this feels like. Feeling the need for value and fulfillment in our lives is often our constant, albeit misunderstood, companion that calls for our attention, our care, and our action.

3. **Each person has a Genius, which is the unique existential DNA passed on to each individual by the creative force. We are "loaded" with our Genius qualities at birth.**

Our consciousness is programmed with our Genius qualities just as our bodies are programmed with the color of our hair, eyes, and skin. The specific difference between our physical and Genius DNA is that often we have to *consciously intend* to express our Genius qualities. They don't necessarily just appear like our physical traits do. Our participation with our Genius is required. As we live and grow, these inborn Genius qualities consistently vie for our conscious attention to be expressed and developed. If we can turn our attention toward them, we can feel them arise in us as a deep feeling of familiarity, or as a mysterious sense of authority and passion about a subject that transcends our logic or explanation. We can also sometimes feel this Genius DNA as a dull or distant ache or longing to express something that feels significant to us. Whichever way they present themselves to us, it is our job to listen and to give our Genius qualities an avenue of expression.

4. **Uncovering our Genius qualities means simply to find the momentum that the universe has already set in motion for us as an expression of itself.**

This momentum of creation is the fuel for our personal existential expression. When we listen deeply to our inner callings, we have the opportunity to use this fuel for our journey and to express our Genius qualities. Instead of carrying the idea that we are struggling alone in the universe to express something unique and valuable, we only need to connect to the original expression of ourselves that has been cast across time and dimension by the creative energy that is sustaining the universe. It had something to express, and our part in that is to continue the expression by adding our personal, conscious effort to it. The impersonal can only go so far in this expression. We have to add the personal to it to allow it to continue to unfold. Like receiving an inheritance from an ancestor, it now becomes our personal task to use the inheritance in our own way, and as it occurs to us.

The intention of the universe was to express something that would then create its own way to continue the expression.

5. **In addition to having an unconscious area of our awareness, we also have a *primaconscious*, where the qualities of our Genius are located. We can access the primaconscious to uncover our Genius callings.**

Like the unconscious or subconscious, there is another layer of consciousness that is the repository of our Genius talents, skills, gifts, and qualities that we have inherited from the original expression of us by Creation. Unlike the unconscious, which holds among other things our shadow material and our psychological woundings, the primaconscious holds the existential DNA of our individual uniqueness. As we go through our lives, the Genius DNA contained in our primaconscious gets activated when we are exposed to an experience, person, or place that resonates with it. At that point we feel our Genius Drive as a source of inspiration, motivation, interest, and vision that gestates an expression from us. This expression comes directly from our Genius. Bringing what is in the primaconscious to the fore helps us to gain a different sense of self and sense of direction based on something that has always belonged to us but has not yet been used or relied upon as our existential inheritance. When we recognize the contents of our primaconscious as a part of our identity to base decisions on, like career, where we live, how we show up in the world, or how we navigate our life transitions, we can make decisions based on elements that are existentially foundational in us. In our effort to heal the woundings contained in our unconscious, we may often neglect this part of our consciousness that has remained intact and whole.

Unlike the unconscious, which is energetically bidirectional, in that it both takes in and expresses psychic and emotional material, the primaconscious is energetically unidirectional. Its expression moves one way: outward. Its purpose is to serve as the foundation for our individual Genius self-expression throughout our lives. Like the energy and direction of a seed, nothing gets stored or collected within it; it is an expressive force moving outward.

It has something to say.

6. **Our Genius and our wounds each have a *drive*, or a fund of energy to express something, and both supply motivation and energy for us to act.**

One well-known explanation of how humans express themselves is Drive Theory, which proposes that we have innate psychological needs that compel or drive us to act, fueled by the buildup of negative tension created from these needs not being met.

My theory identifies two basic drives that pertain to self-expression: the Wound Drive and the Genius Drive, which are fueled by differing energetic sources. In short, the Wound Drive moves us towards healing and returning to the wholeness of what was wounded within us, while the Genius Drive moves toward the expression of something new that is held within us in potential.

THE GENIUS DRIVE

I have found, by working closely with people across the spectrums of culture, socioeconomics, gender, and age, that each person has what I call an individual **Genius Drive** with a particular collection of interests that feel important and therefore motivating to them to express. The Genius Drive as a motivator to act pertains directly to a person's life direction and purpose. This drive isn't a buildup of negative tension, but instead is a storehouse of unexpressed potential given to the individual by existence as an identity to be expressed in their lifetime. Think of the "fierce energy" stored in the acorn from earlier in this book.

My work with clients has shown me that it is not the interest or activity itself that is motivating, but the inbuilt *connection* to the interest or activity in the person's Genius Drive that makes it so. Therefore, it doesn't matter what the interest or activity is; it matters only that it feels important to the individual to express.

The hallmark of Genius isn't about being better than others at something; it's about getting better at expressing the inborn qualities contained in your own Genius.

Connecting to your own Genius Drive generates a type of motivation that surpasses outside-based inspiration. The energy contained in your Genius Drive is inexhaustible because it is the part of you that was given by existence itself. This means that existence has a stake in your expressing what's in your Genius.

Another way to express this idea is that Creation wants to express itself as you, and it has packed that potential expression with all of the energy, motivation, and means necessary to express it. Since our Genius Drive has an agenda—

basically *is* an agenda to express something in particular—it reminds us of its existence within us over and over again. What this reminder feels like can range from a sense of vital urgency to express something in particular to "hearing" a small voice calling us repeatedly from an unknown depth; from a feeling of dissatisfaction or dullness with how we're currently living to an existential ache that feels critical to soothe.

THE WOUND DRIVE

The other major drive at play pertaining to self-expression is what I've identified as the **Wound Drive**. This drive is fueled by the need to repair or heal an aspect of ourselves that has been emotionally or psychologically wounded, damaged, or impaired at some point in our life.

Each one of us without exception has these types of wounds that insistently call for their healing. Some, of course, are more difficult to heal than others, depending on the severity of the wound, as in the case of trauma. For many of us, the Wound Drive is the primary drive motivating our actions. It is largely unconscious, meaning that it is operating without our being consciously aware of it, but has such a great need for healing that it appears daily as a source of motivation and direction. The significant distinction to make between the expressions of the Genius Drive and the Wound Drive is that they have divergent goals. Simply stated, the Wound Drive wants to heal, repair, or return to a healthy state of wholeness, while the Genius Drive wants to fulfill an existential task of expressing something new. Both bring the motivation to self-express, but move down specific paths that lead to different destinations and outcomes.

The Genius Way process shows how to discern the difference between these two drives in your own awareness so you can be clear about where the motivating energy you're using to self-express is actually leading you. It's either to a place of healing or to a new expression of yourself. Both destinations are good; they're just different.

The reason it's important to know which drive your motivation is coming from is so you actually end up where you want to be going. For example, if you feel inspired and motivated to create a nonprofit foundation that addresses the plight of undocumented immigrants, and your personal wounds occurred around that issue, creating your foundation can be healing for you. Your Genius may even be activated in the effort and will serve to create a foundation that is truly unique. That is a wonderful process, but the important distinction to make is that our Genius is not simply a tool to heal our wounds. Conversely, if one of your Genius qualities is to bring public awareness to a cause, and you use this talent to create this same foundation, you will experience a sense of fulfillment of purpose that is uniquely different in feeling tone than the feeling of healing a wound. It is like the difference between the feeling of returning home and the feeling of presenting something new to the world that is uniquely you. Both are good, and both are necessary. They simply serve different purposes and need to be acknowledged for what they are.

Remember that Genius is the seed of self-expression given to us by existence, and that it had its own task to express something long before our woundings ever happened. It has its own agenda to share something unique with the world. So if your need for self-expression is not about healing a wound, but about expressing something new that feels important to you, connecting with your Genius Drive is the key.

To be clear: It is vitally important to work through our psychological woundings by corrective cognitions, actions, and expressions. This healing is valuable and necessary work. There are countless books, models, and theories on how to do that, and a large part of my function as a therapist is to help my clients come to terms with and work through their psychological wounds in our sessions.

The Genius Way is a different approach in that it focuses on the non-wounded Genius self that we were born with, bringing it forward so it can express something new. This new expression, which comes from the depths of our primaconscious state of awareness, is healing in a different sense; it allows us to see an intrinsic value in ourself that predates our childhood story and consequently our woundings. To identify with the Genius qualities that you were born with puts healing your wounds into a clearer perspective. If you discover that you were born with something specific to express, and tasked by existence to do so, then suddenly the goal of your life isn't just about healing all of your childhood wounds or traumatic experiences, but also to make sure that your inborn gifts get expressed outwardly. You're not just a wounded person trying to become whole; you are a whole and resourced person from the start, with your own Genius expression, who experienced some wounding. Healing our wounds and expressing our Genius are equally but separately important.

7. **Our current *life expression* pertains to which drive, Genius or Wound, is motivating our actions, choices, and behavior in the present moment.**

As a manifest expression of the creative force, we, *as* this expression, combined with our free will, are constantly "saying something" with our life as a whole. This is important to know, because our life expression is the framework from which we move through our life, make decisions, interact with others, and exercise our values and principles. Depending on which expression drive we're acting or expressing from, Wound or Genius, our actions carry the motivational energy, direction, and goal of that particular drive. Bringing your conscious awareness to which drive framework you're operating from can help you to create the situation and outcome that you actually want to happen.

LIFE CAN BE LIVED WITH A SENSE OF PURPOSE

The idea of living your life with a sense of direction and purpose isn't meant to be some unreachable ideal or a watered-down inspirational meme that pops up in your social media feed. One reason that the idea of living with direction and purpose has continued throughout human experience is that it has its roots in a solid and basic principle: Higher-order human needs will appear in our awareness after the primary needs for food, shelter, and safety have been fulfilled. We can't turn them off, because they're part of us. These built-in higher-order needs actually drive us to search for a purpose to our lives. To recognize life purpose as a human need, and to actually feel your individual need for life direction and purpose, is essential to the continuation of your life journey.

LIFE PURPOSE COMES FROM EXPRESSING OUR GENIUS SELVES

The Genius Way is a framework or way of navigating your life based on the idea that we all have a Genius self—a particular set of callings or inborn gifts that are natural for us to express with our lives. This isn't a new idea. Most people would agree that every one of us possesses at least some specific qualities that make us unique. However, unless we take that idea and become conscientious and committed to finding our own Genius self, our lives may continue to feel purposeless and directionless.

Finding and identifying the callings contained in your Genius self can shift the perspective you hold toward yourself and the world you live in. The Genius Way is a framework that creates a life practice of seeing and engaging with your life from that perspective; life decisions, forward movement, and personal choices are made from the wisdom gained from understanding your individual Genius.

Genius qualities can be recognized, uncovered, tended to, and expressed. When life is seen from the Genius perspective, it becomes an adventure to participate with, or a set of opportunities to experiment with, on the path of your unique human expression.

TAKING LIFE PURPOSE EARNESTLY

Life direction and meaning are found by those who listen, look, and make their Genius callings a priority. They are following the call of a voice that is connected to the creative universe itself, which has been there all along, though largely unnoticed and unexpressed.

It's one thing not to have any potential for a meaningful life. It's quite another thing to have the potential for living with direction and purpose in the marrow of your existence and to not be aware of it. Listening to the voice of our Genius and our life callings is a deliberate act. And the closer we listen, the more we feel the importance of expressing what we're hearing.

Considering that our Genius callings are meant to be expressed, and by us in particular, we have to deliberately spend our time on them to bring them forward for expression.

The Genius Way process is a way of doing just that. It is a way of deliberately spending your time uncovering your Genius callings.

MAKING GENIUS A PART OF YOUR LIFE

Living with a conscious awareness of your Genius in your life isn't going to happen by accident. With so many pulls on our attention and awareness from our wounded self that is trying to heal, our Genius all too often goes unnoticed and unexplored. Part of my effort with this book is to reinforce the idea that life purpose and expressing our Genius selves is a *human need*—indeed, the individual task with which we are charged—rather than an indulgence or an extravagance.

The Genius Way process provides the essential skills to uncover your own Genius callings, express them, and tend to your Genius. Each of the ten Life Skill chapters teaches you an essential life skill that you'll use to make your inborn Genius a part of your everyday life.

THE GENIUS WAY FRAMEWORK

IN LEARNING HOW TO consciously participate with and express our Genius, we have to place ourselves in a context or **_framework of practice_** that prioritizes our Genius expression. The Genius Way process is such a framework, one that supports your Genius identity.

Let's return to our seed metaphor to illustrate how a Genius-based framework can become a part of your everyday life.

A primary function of any seed is to seek out a further expression of the initial expression; the acorn unfolds its inner potential to become the oak. Trunk, branches, and leaves gradually emerge from its unseen identity into the material world. Likewise, a primary function of our Genius is to seek out further expression of the initial trove of gifts and qualities we were born with. It is a natural phenomenon to unfold and exhibit what is initially unseen in us. Our life callings and individual self-expression emerge from our unseen Genius identity as our unique contribution to the world around us.

This part is *impersonal*.

Acorn or Genius, existence colludes to help the further expression to happen. This means that the acorn doesn't need to worry about whether it has what it takes to become an oak. That is its primary function. What it already *is* is enough to complete the task, and there's no question about it.

The Genius Way proposes that, like the acorn, humans already have within us the essence of what we need to live a rich and fulfilling life. Unlike the acorn, however, we humans have to *personalize* our journey, meaning that we must deliberately choose to align our actions and expression with our inborn Genius that contains the seed of our life direction and purpose. We can take the position that, just like the acorn, we already possess in potential what it takes to live with a sense of meaning and purpose. But to make sure we are working with, and not against, our own nature, we need to consciously participate with our own Genius and its callings. **We are tasked with co-creating our lives.**

A seed is a paradox. It is simultaneously complete and incomplete, at once finished *and* in flux. If a seed doesn't root into the earth and transform into the next expression of itself, arguably it will remain physically intact and complete *as a seed*. But the *potential* in the seed—the possibility of the more mature manifestation it can become—needs to be imagined or dreamt into existence. By taking the step of planting itself in the earth, it isn't doing so because something or someone gave it a guarantee that it would grow. It is acting more on a feeling or a hunch that this is the right thing for it to do. Without a promise of success, this first expression of a seed needs to be *risked* in order to achieve the next expression. The invisible potential that the seed feels inside itself allows it to take the initial chance of burying its present complete version in the earth to become the next and fuller version.

We, as human seeds, exist simultaneously as our Genius selves and wounded selves, at once connected and disconnected from our existential heritage. We hold this paradox within us throughout the entirety of our lives. To further the expression of our individual Genius, we first have to *risk giving up* the core belief or narrative of ourselves as individuals who live disconnected from existence and are born without a personal inner compass to guide and direct us. When we take the risk of letting go of this intact but false concept of ourselves as a disconnected individual for the sake of stepping into the larger concept of being a connected individual with a Genius that has something to express, we are creating the internal space needed for a deeper capacity of understanding, growth, and possibility.

Besides its DNA and potential, a seed also needs a supportive environment or *framework* within which to grow into the further expression of itself. Earth, water, sun, and seasons make up the framework that has supported every seed's growth for millennia. It has no need to worry or doubt its capability to grow; it just needs its basic nature and the proper framework.

Your Genius's further expression of itself needs to be supported by its own kind of framework, made up of, among other things, the core beliefs and personal narratives that you hold individually.

Most of us operate from a set of unconscious personal assumptions that rest on our psychological experiences and woundings, but don't include the presence of our Genius. This framework may be sufficient to move through our lives with the aim of healing our personal psychologies but is inadequate in supporting the expression of our Genius.

To support a Genius-based life, we need a framework that is comprised of core beliefs, concepts, values, principles, tools, and practices that directly pertain to the existence, encouragement, and maintenance of our inner Genius. And we need to *consciously* adopt this framework on a personal level to creatively contribute and participate with what our Genius is here to express.

Therefore, the Genius Way process begins with this basic idea:

> Your Genius self rightly exists.
>
> It feels meaningful and fulfilling to identify your Genius and express it.
>
> From your Genius identity you have something valuable to contribute to the world around you while you are here.

THE GENIUS WAY FRAMEWORK

As we live our lives, we all are required to place whatever we are doing, seeing, or approaching into a context, or frame of reference. We do it out of necessity, because as humans we need to position ourselves somewhere in the current story in which we find ourselves to create a sense of self.

For example, as a child, and like most children, I borrowed my parents' frame of reference, which included things like my nationality, religion, family history, and emotional modeling. Their framework became mine, and I was able to develop and know myself as a separate person within this structure.

In adolescence, as I was exposed to more societal influences, I chose a different frame that helped me to make sense of my more expanded experience of the world, and which gave me a different way to navigate the experiences and input that I was encountering at the time. As we grow, change, and age, we find ourselves needing new frames of reference by which we can meet our current challenges and situations more successfully.

In my late teens I was struggling with my sense of self and trying to build an identity that was large enough to hold my hopes and dreams for the future. Like many in my generation who were looking for deeper meaning in their lives, I embraced a spiritual lifestyle, adopting an Eastern-based framework and philosophy, using elements of Hinduism, Buddhism, and Taoism. It felt refreshing to be practicing a new paradigm that had personal enlightenment as its goal.

For many years this framework was large and new enough to help me to develop cognitively and emotionally, and it provided me a sense of life purpose and meaning. At some point, however, the new framework I had embraced became too small for me; that is to say, I had unknowingly outgrown it. I began feeling trapped in the context that years before had been my salvation.

The thing about frameworks is that we can and *do* outgrow them. They are essentially the psychological and conceptual clothes we wear for a certain time, until our body of experience and wisdom needs larger garments to clothe and house the more expansive person we have now become. The old frame served us well, as our childhood clothing had served us. But unlike the outgrown clothes from our past that were easily discarded, we often hold onto our life frames far past their usefulness. The feelings of discomfort and dissatisfaction with our lives as we remain in an outdated framework are messages from our Genius that we need to make a change. We feel the tightness, the stress, the wear of something that doesn't fit anymore, but we haven't been taught that we should listen to these feelings as a signal that we can and should discard an old framework when something new is needed.

The education of how to consciously create a new self-framework is essential to finding our life direction and expressing our Genius.

Whichever frame we choose to use, we need to make sure that the frame is large enough to hold our current conception of the world and our place in it. It has to have extra room for us to continue to grow. It needs to be able to contain our values and principles, our dreams for the future, and our idea of what part our past plays in our life. It needs to be large enough to hold all of the existential supplies we will need for our journey forward toward our chosen life goals: vision, inspiration, encouragement, hopefulness. A purposive frame should be able to accommodate all of this. If your current life framework doesn't have room for this kind of growth, it just isn't big enough. You can know this by how it feels to you to be living within it.

If you have the courage to be honest with yourself about how your current life framework feels to you, you'll be able to make the much-needed change. Often we must give ourselves permission to shed a framework we have loved, but have outgrown.

Your Genius-based framework needs to be consciously put into place with the awareness that it can and will need to be modified in the future as you gain self-awareness and deepen your experience as a connected individual.

If acorns possessed rational minds, and if someone were to explain the journeys they would have to take to become oaks, there would certainly be fewer trees on Earth! The idea of risking their complete and intact "acornness" to become something more, merely on the idea that they will grow from their humble form into something much larger and more developed, might seem too dangerous or silly for many of them.

Since as humans we do have minds that rationalize and reason, we must not rely on these qualities alone to help us choose to listen to our inner Genius callings or to motivate us to change our current life expression into one that expresses Genius. Rational thought will always stay with the first intact expression, however uncomfortable, because there is no outward guarantee that the seed of Genius in us will grow into something more fulfilling and meaningful. Instead, we can respond with another aspect of ourselves and follow the *sense* and *feeling* within us that without the next, fuller expression of unfolding our Genius selves, the existential task we've been given just hasn't been done; the potential we've been born with hasn't been expressed. That feeling isn't going to go away. Your Genius exists and will consistently let you know that it is ready to grow.

THE THREE PRINCIPLES OF THE GENIUS WAY FRAMEWORK

The Genius Way process is based upon three solid principles that can help you to create a healthy, Genius-based life with purposeful direction and a sense of personal meaning. In each of the ten life skill chapters of the Genius Way process, you will be using these three principles to create your Genius-based life. Let's discuss these three principles in more detail.

INSIGHT

As a therapist and teacher, I've spent much of my life and career helping others gain insights about their own psychological conditions and spiritual journeys. Many therapists work in this way, and so most of us are operating under the concept that having a deep insight will be the key element in bringing about the changes and transformations we are wanting in our lives.

In my professional and personal experience, this is only partially true.

Insight is absolutely necessary. It can shed the light of understanding on our dark places and bring a life-affirming perspective to the issues we are facing. It can appear as a sudden satori, "aha" moment, or enlightenment, and through its perspective-shifting power, a deep insight can position us to make great strides towards a life path that is healthier and more congruous with our Genius.

We all know what having an insight feels like. Insight gives us a glimpse of what our lives can become. The vision comes upon us suddenly—like an awakening or revelation. Insight serves as the clarion bell for the rest of the journey of realization. But unless we have a framework in which to shape a part of our life around that insight, or to grow further into it, it will remain as an experience that happened to us at one point in time, and with every passing moment the potency of it will recede further into the past.

In the ten steps of the Genius Way process, you'll be gaining insight from mining your primaconscious for content and clues about your own Genius self, with its callings, talents, and gifts. These insights can be seen as doors that open for you to walk through. They are the beginnings of what can turn out to be your path of expressing your Genius self.

Insight alone isn't what gets the job done, however. An insight is like a small spark that needs to be initially protected and given fuel to become a flame large enough to cast ongoing light and warmth. After having an insight, we need to take action to protect and feed the small spark, or else it can dwindle and fade. Conversely, we extinguish the potency of an insight by not engaging with it.

To acknowledge our insights for the gifts they are, and for them to take root and grow within us, we need to have an expressive response to them. The expressive response is a way of crystallizing the importance of the insight. A symbolic action must be taken to bring the insight across the threshold of our interiority into our outer life framework. In this way we are honoring the gift of new perspective that has dawned in us; we take care of it wholeheartedly because in our search for a sense of meaning, purpose, or direction, we had originally asked for something, and when the insight came to us, we were answered. Taking an action or making an expression in response is to acknowledge the answer that we've received. In this way we are dialoging with existence via our responsive self-expression.

For example, let's say that you don't consider yourself a morning person, and it's hard for you to get your day started. You find yourself wishing that you could have a more positive and hopeful attitude when you wake up. One morning you see a text from an old friend on your phone. It makes you smile to remember and feel connected to your friend. Floating on this feeling of connection, your morning feels positive and hopeful. You feel one of your Genius qualities, the ability to maintain deep, long-standing friendships, come to the surface of your awareness, and you write a heartfelt email to some other close friends to tell them how much you appreciate their presence in your life. This too is a Genius quality, you realize: you often facilitate connections between others. After an hour, you realize that this morning you feel really good about being awake. The insight comes to you that the feeling of being connected to your friend and the part of your Genius it summoned up actually changed your morning experience. In this way, your wish for a way to feel more positive was answered. And the insight was accompanied by the key to creating that circumstance in the future.

There are two steps to crystallizing and protecting an insight. Both of these steps are conscious responses; they are actions or intentions that make us engaged participants in the process of furthering existence's initial expression of us.

The first response to an insight is to make a *commitment* to its manifestation in your life.

This leads us to the second principle of the Genius Way process: commitment.

COMMITMENT

Living a Genius-based life is about committing to uncover your own Genius qualities by giving your insights time and space to develop and grow. Commitment in this context is to recognize the fact that you have a Genius self and that you are committed to prioritizing it in your day-to-day life. Commitment to your Genius self is what will allow you to return to your center and ground yourself throughout your continued development. It's what serves as a constant reminder of how you've chosen to live your life in the small moments of time. It's said that your true character is displayed by how you live and act when no one is watching you. Similarly, whatever you are committed to will silently motivate the decisions and actions you take in your expressive life. Making a conscious daily commitment to expressing your Genius is how you make sure that your inner gifts and qualities don't remain hidden and unexplored.

Making a commitment to something makes things simple. Once you commit, it becomes the default action to remember what you committed to, and to return to it again and again when you feel lost, confused, or disoriented with your life path. It becomes the conscious habit that you practice and develop to keep you on track as your life continuously moves into the future.

Let's follow the previous example of an insight about how expressing gratitude for your connectedness to others brought out your Genius and changed your morning experience. A commitment would be to consciously decide to spend a short time every morning to think of the people you share love with in your life—those who bring you joy or make you smile. Remember that your Genius wants to express, and the expression that changed your morning experience was one of connection. Making a commitment to feel the gratitude of being connected to your friends each morning will give your Genius an avenue of expression for that life-changing quality of yourself that was uncovered as a result of your insight. A commitment allows your insight to take root in your outer expressive world. You recognize that your Genius lies in eliciting and facilitating interconnectedness among those you know and love. Your deep feeling of connection to others feeds your ability to be of service as a "connector" as the opportunity arises.

PRACTICE

The second response to an insight is to create a *practice* around it, so the insight can be nurtured and allowed to grow into its potential. To create a practice from an insight is to set aside some time each day to acknowledge the insight by doing something differently or in addition to what you had been doing before the insight occurred.

One of the great and simple truths about the human experience is that our lives become about whatever we spend most of our time doing. Each of us has only been given an indeterminate and limited amount of time. What we choose to do with our time actually shapes us into who we become in the world. Spending our allotted amount of time on something is to prioritize that thing, and therefore is a statement of what we have deemed most important in our lives.

For many of us, this prioritization process is unconscious. For example, we may unknowingly be prioritizing safety and security by working from a low-grade state of fear or anxiety every day. In that case, every day we're practicing how to be scared and anxious. Conversely, using our time to consciously prioritize things like trust and gratitude can allow us to practice working in a relaxed state, which makes us better at welcoming good and rewarding experiences into our lives. With each day of practice, we're getting better and stronger at whatever we're practicing.

The Genius Way process is a practice of prioritizing our Genius gifts and callings, so that we get better and better at expressing our Genius every day. We do this by spending our valuable time acknowledging the things that make our life feel purposeful and meaningful. We keep our sights on the quality of our life experience in this present moment, knowing that how we live in this moment will set us up for the next moment, and the next moment, and so on.

The practice of expressing your Genius self is to trust your insight, commit to your Genius callings, and orient yourself to align with them throughout your day as you make your decisions, interact with others, and spend your allotted time.

Using the previous example, to take your commitment to feel grateful every morning to a practice level, you could choose to begin each day by actively remembering and acknowledging your connections with the people you love. You may wish to rise, wash your face, and then sit with eyes closed for five or ten minutes, feeling gratitude for loved ones past and present. This practice is rooted in your insight and grounded in your commitment, and therefore has the best possible chance of being a self-expression that yields positive feelings. This in turn strengthens your Genius for forging deep friendships and, by extension, helping others to form or maintain connections, to their mutual benefit. Remember that whatever you practice becomes stronger each time you do it, and you will get better and better at it with each passing day. You may find new clarity in the ways you are able to serve others that comes to you throughout your day following your morning practice.

THE GENIUS WAY PROCESS

IN THE GENIUS WAY framework, finding and expressing our Genius selves is seen as a developmental stage given to each one of us by existence itself.

My experience as a therapist and teacher has helped me to identify ten key life skills to learn and develop that can help us move through and accomplish this existential developmental stage or task. By learning and using these essential life skills, we can create a life based on our innate Genius callings. These ten life skills are represented by the ten workbook-style chapters that follow in the Genius Way process.

The word education comes from the Latin word *educare*, which means to *lead out* or *raise up*. In order to help you to flesh out your Genius so it becomes a living reality in your day-to-day life, each workbook chapter is designed to educate you and "lead out" your Genius. With each chapter, you will learn a new life skill and build on your awareness of your own Genius and Genius Drive. These are skills that you can embody and take into your life as you move forward into your future. This set of skills helps you identify the subtle changes you can make in your moment-to-moment existence that will raise and bring your Genius qualities forward. In this way they become part of your conscious expression instead of existing somewhere in the background of your awareness.

The Genius Way process is designed to be a *self-generated* protocol to inform and direct you on your individual life path. That means that the information you will use on this journey will be coming from your inner world and environment. Each section of this book is designed to bring your Genius self into higher focus, primarily by mining content from your primaconscious and then working with what you find there. The idea is for you to discover what is already present within you as your existential DNA and to access your inner resources for expressing your Genius self in this lifetime. You will learn how to listen to your Genius callings and develop practical ways to use your inner gifts as a guide and compass to move forward in your life. You will be able to refer to them when you need to find life direction, make life choices, and stay on track with your life goals.

The Genius Way process is a journey of change. As part of that change, you will be discovering hidden aspects of yourself that are rarely discerned by ordinary life experiences. By taking a direct and purposive look at the level of yourself where your Genius exists, you'll find a part of your deeper identity that has been with you all along, but perhaps was not accessed or relied upon for your everyday functioning.

The mission of the Genius Way is to elicit your hidden Genius qualities so you can bring your Genius gifts into the world.

UNCONDITIONAL POSITIVE SELF-REGARD

Carl Rogers, who was one of the founders of humanistic psychology, used the term *unconditional positive regard* as a way of describing a healing approach in which a client who comes for therapy is simply accepted unconditionally, regardless of what the person says or does in their sessions. This creates a safe and healing environment or therapeutic container to work within. Many therapists today use this approach in their work. During the Genius Way process, I'm going to ask you to use this concept of unconditional positive regard with yourself. Using unconditional positive *self*-regard when going through a process like the Genius Way is imperative in creating a safe and healthy space from which you can evolve and grow.

Let's take a moment to consider how unconditional positive self-regard would look and function in our lives.

One thing that many of my clients never consider is that they should fact-check what their critical mind says about them. Many of us don't even consider that we're allowed to! For the most part, we accept our negative and critical self-narratives as gospel, since they are coming from "inside" us and therefore appear to be "our voice." We don't ever think to challenge or correct them. We then allow the negative story to be the backdrop for our sense of self, never realizing that we are actually fighting with ourselves and not the outside world when it comes to creating healthy and fulfilling lives.

For example:

James was an intelligent and responsible husband and father, who ran a business and supported his family both financially and emotionally. In fact, he was responsible to a fault, due to his particular childhood trauma around a chaotic and unsafe home environment. Out of necessity, he had taken it upon himself to hold his family of origin together at a very young age. But instead of living with the satisfaction of actually accomplishing this herculean feat, he carried a severely critical self-narrative, internalized from parental voices in childhood, that he was stupid, careless, and ineffective. It wasn't until we exposed this habitual self-narrative that he was able to begin to check it for accuracy, appreciate the abundant evidence to the contrary, and eventually reject this critical self-narrative as false.

The fact is, we *can* create a healthy, supportive, and loving sense of self and self-care. Many of us just weren't taught how to do this. Yes, we may carry an unconscious negative belief that causes us to not feel good enough about ourselves in some way. If we think we're too much of one thing, or not enough of another, we may secretly and silently harbor the feeling of falling short as a person. This path will never lead to a fulfilling life. Somehow, and at some time, if we want our lives to change for the better, we will have to take another path on which we're consciously choosing a self-supportive narrative.

That time for you is likely right now. You are reading this book for a reason. You're looking for something. My position is that whatever attracted you to this book and is motivating you to read it is an extremely valuable part of yourself. It deserves to be taken seriously and respected. As you move through the Genius Way process, I'm going to ask you to regard yourself the way I do, with validation and unconditional acceptance.

Approach your own need to have a clear and focused life direction with a sense of purpose as valuable, important, deserved, and worthwhile.

Put on the mantle of earnestness and sincerity while you practice this self-awareness work.

Set apart this time as a sacred time for yourself.

Do it for this one significant life that you have right now.

THE TEN LIFE SKILL CHAPTERS

EACH LIFE SKILL CHAPTER has seven sections, designed to help you easily move through the Genius Way process. Let's take a look at each section and learn how they work.

CHECK IN

We begin each new life skill chapter by checking in: acknowledging anything that you found particularly important from the previous chapter and want to remember and reinforce as you go forward. Checking in will help you to look closely at how you are moving through the Genius Way process and to name the thoughts and feelings that are making up your experience so far. It's a way of keeping track of where you've been and where you're going.

STUDENT/CLIENT STORY

In this section I give a real-life example of one of my clients' or students' stories and how we worked together using the Genius Way process. The issue in each story represents the life skill that is being taught in that chapter.

NEW LEARNING

Next is a short teaching about the life skill covered in the chapter. It is designed to educate and "raise up" any latent curiosities and interests about your Genius that will be developed further during the Guided Content-Mining section of each lesson chapter.

GUIDED CONTENT-MINING

This section will allow you to mine content from your primaconscious. Through a guided journey, you will bring up information contained in your Genius DNA to use in the next section, the Insight Protocol. You will access your primaconscious for the qualities of your Genius that it contains. Instead of bringing content from your unconscious, you'll tap into your primaconscious to bring out your gifts, talents, and callings. This effort is not about healing wounds from your past. Its purpose is to set you on the path of expressing something new: the potential contained in your Genius. You may wish to listen to the audio version of the guided exercise on www.thegeniusway.com/guidedexercises, or read one sentence at a time, then close your eyes and follow the visuals that arise.

USING THE GENIUS WAY INSIGHT PROTOCOL

After the content-mining exercise, you'll have uncovered an insight from the psychic material you've brought to conscious awareness. Instead of leaving it there, you'll strengthen and deepen your connection to your insight by using the Genius Way Insight Protocol. The Insight Protocol is a five-step process to ground you into what you've self-discovered.

The Insight Protocol enables you to document the primaconscious material and experiences you uncover and bring to conscious awareness. Over the course of the ten life skill chapters, using the Insight Protocol prompts, you will collect and curate the insights you receive, taking note of the images and feelings that arise in the process. When you finish all ten chapters, you'll scan their content for repeated themes and insights that arise. This will inform you about your individual Genius qualities in a concrete way.

One of the interesting things I've encountered while working with students and clients throughout the years is a commonly held belief that having an insight or sudden realization is transformative in and of itself. Most people believe that having a realization will magically change them into a new person who will make better decisions, break old habits, and live with a sense of purpose and direction. Sadly, this is not at all accurate.

I have found repeatedly that insight is only the first part of creating lasting personal change. For transformation to happen—that is to say, for *lasting* change to happen—our insight needs to be tended to and worked with in a purposive way.

From the Genius Way perspective, receiving an insight is truly a gift and opportunity for growth. Insights don't come by accident and always appear at the right time. An insight is a message for us that has come from our interiority and our connected self to enhance, improve, or develop our life in some way. Caring and tending to our insights is a way of responding to existence in a way that says that we have received the message and that we are listening to our deeper selves as a source of information and direction. Strengthening our ability to listen to ourselves in this deep way is to develop an inner skill that relies on the intuition that comes directly from our Genius.

THE GENIUS WAY INSIGHT PROTOCOL HAS FIVE STEPS:

Step 1. Acknowledge the insight.

First, acknowledge the insight by writing it down. For example, you might write, "In my guided journey I saw that every time I sing, I feel like I am who I am meant to be." Documenting your insight is the first step into real-izing your insight by bringing it from the inside to the outside; you are taking the first step of manifestation by writing it down. You are making it real.

Step 2. Find an image.

Next, find an inner image that embodies the insight. Let's say from your insight you see an image of yourself standing on a stage and singing. Go into the image and notice everything you can about it. Where is the stage? How many people are watching you? What are you singing? What time of day is it? And so on. Write down everything you see and hear in the image.

Step 3. Find the seed feeling in the image.

Now, search the image for a feeling contained within it. Every image is packed full of information, including a *seed feeling* of what the image promises you'll feel when you attain it. For example, using the image of singing on a stage, describe what that experience feels like. You may identify a feeling of fulfillment, acknowledgment, using your full potential, joy, etc. This is your seed feeling contained in the image and represents what you are wanting to feel in the future. This seed feeling is an indicator and a guide to you as you walk your Genius path. It is part of your Genius DNA and will help you to recognize the people, places, and experiences that support your Genius by how it feels when you are close to them. Giving your insight dimensionality by acknowledging the feeling aspect makes it a more substantial part of your life, so it becomes easier to remember and strengthen as you move through your day. Experiencing the seed feeling of your insight will help you make it real.

Step 4. Make a commitment to express this aspect of your Genius.

Use this section to make a commitment to your Genius self to remember what was just mined from your primaconscious and to use it in your life. Without a commitment, your insight never moves into expression. A commitment can also be seen as an intention or a decision. Just as you might set an intention or make a decision to walk north instead of south, a commitment entails taking a stand and picking a direction in which to head to express your Genius. And remember, expressing your Genius is what allows you to create or change your life direction.

The reason I have put a commitment section in each chapter is that committing ourselves to a task only works when the commitment is ongoing and supported by a practice. You can think of a commitment as the intellectual and emotional decision to change that fuels a new behavior from you. Taking the time every day to stop and acknowledge your commitment to your Genius self is a necessary step to make your practice stick.

Step 5. Practice. Make a symbolic action.

The next step is to develop a small practice around your insight, image, and seed feeling. Here you will set yourself up to practice your new life skill by *acting* on the insight you gained in the content-mining section. The first four steps brought your insight into clearer focus. To continue and solidify your insight into your daily life, you'll need to spend time with it, and the best way to do that is to practice something that will deepen and strengthen the connection to the insight. It doesn't have to be an elaborate or time-consuming effort. Just enough to acknowledge and tend to the insight by giving it a small amount of your time and attention during your day.

With a practice, you are creating or changing your momentum; telling your brain to create new neural pathways based on your conscious choices; and strengthening those neural pathways every day. They then become the new way that you function, choose, and respond in your life.

Making a symbolic action while you are freshly aware of your primaconscious Genius qualities is how you begin to open an avenue of expression and practice. The symbolic action is the first step to bringing your primaconscious Genius material into the physical world, pulling it over the threshold from the inner to the outer, and making it more accessible for you to express and relate to as a part of yourself. It also breaks the ice into the question of how expressing your Genius is possible. A symbolic action can be as simple as standing up, writing something down, picking up a book, expressing a dream out loud, etc.

DOUBTS

This section is for acknowledging any self-doubt about your Genius and any skepticism or cynicism about the work you're doing to uncover it. Don't worry, it won't kill your buzz.

Doubts are fine. They're just thoughts that are attached to emotions. Acknowledging our doubts allows us to distinguish them from our intuitions or gut feelings. When we can make space even for our doubts, we no longer have to fight with them or let them distract us from what we're doing. The trouble with having doubts comes when we don't examine them for accuracy, and then allow them to be the last voice of authority that makes our decisions for us. The fact is, our doubts are only one part of our awareness and should be regarded from that perspective.

A psychological tool for working with doubts is to use Parts Theory. That means to see your doubts as they arise, name them, and give them a voice as a part of you. For example, if you have the doubt that your Genius even exists, acknowledge it, name it the "I don't have a Genius" doubt, and say something as if this doubt is speaking: "Your Genius doesn't exist." Or if you doubt whether you have any value as an individual, name it the "No value" doubt, and write down a sentence in the voice of this doubt: "You are worthless." When you can acknowledge your doubts as a *part* of you, they no longer have the power to stop the *whole* of you that does include the feeling that your Genius is real and that you are individually valuable. In this way, when a doubt arises, your position is just, "Oh, there's a doubt, I know that one. Now let me keep going." Having a doubt doesn't shut down your operation. You get to choose which part of you guides your actions, choices, and behavior.

In the Doubts section, take the time to write down any doubts that are occurring to you about your current experience.

AFFIRMATIONS

In this section, I offer some encouraging affirmations to help you on your personal Genius way until the next chapter. Repeating these to yourself, either aloud or silently, can help you point your conscious awareness in the direction of your Genius self.

PERSONAL CONTENT

You'll use this space to collect and curate the experiential information you've uncovered in each life skill chapter, so it's all in one place. After you've completed all ten chapters of the process, you'll go to what you've written from each chapter and circle or highlight any thoughts, feelings, or images that repeat or stand out to you throughout your work. Then you'll take these recurring words or sentences and write them in the Personal Content section. From there, you'll distill what you've written into one or two sentences that potently sum up and contain the essence of what you've discovered about your Genius self.

As you move through the Genius Way process, you will have realizations about yourself that will continue to deepen and open up further over time. Make sure not to rush through the Life Skill chapters and exercises. Instead, give your realizations and insights time to open up in your awareness and reveal their richness and fullness by going back to the exercises that feel particularly important to you. Trust how your feelings guide you to linger or return to a particular life skill or exercise. Remember that your Genius is being activated here, and it has its own priorities and agenda. Take your time and listen to what you are drawn to as you move through the book.

HOW TO USE THIS BOOK

- Use your unconditional positive self-regard; don't judge your process or discoveries.

- In addition to writing your primaconscious content, feel free to draw or sketch any images, impressions, or doodles that come to you as you move through the exercises.

- Take your time and return to any life skill chapter that feels important to you, to mine more of your primaconscious Genius content.

THE TEN LIFE SKILLS
OF THE GENIUS WAY

LIFE SKILL ONE —
Naming your Genius and
Making It Part of Your Daily Life

CHECK IN

Now that you've looked over the basic concepts and steps of the Genius Way philosophy, it's time to make it personal by using the Genius Way process to develop and practice the life skills you'll need to make your individual Genius a foundational piece of your everyday life and identity.

As you begin, remember to give yourself the greatest advantage possible for success by practicing unconditional positive self-regard. Your nonjudgmental attitude of acceptance will set the proper inner tone for this first chapter, which teaches you how to name your Genius and bring conscious awareness to its existence within you.

CLIENT STORY

Ryan was a stay-at-home dad with two children. He came to see me to work through some anxiety issues stemming from childhood experiences. His anxiety had spilled into the area of his family life, where the basic tasks of running a household often left him feeling uninspired and purposeless. Being an extremely conscientious and sincere person, he was struggling to understand why he wasn't able to derive a greater sense of fulfillment from cooking meals and keeping a clean house for his family. Although he loved being a father and husband, he felt that his life was lacking something extremely important to him.

In one of our sessions, Ryan began to speak about a social issue that was happening in his local community, and I noticed that he was suddenly excited, engaged, interested, energized, and speaking with a sense of authority—all hallmarks of his Genius self being activated. Suddenly, on this topic, his intelligence and innate interest and curiosity were being expressed in a way that was natural for him, and the time he spent describing his ideas felt important and fulfilling.

I asked Ryan to acknowledge the accompanying energy, enthusiasm, passion, and purpose he felt every time he was working with this issue in some way, and to name this combination of feelings and energy as his Genius Drive. To keep the focus on *identifying* his Genius—and rather than trying to immediately imagine a career or a way to profit from the discovery of this aspect of himself—we simply took notice that his Genius Drive contained energetic potential around identifying a social issue and exploring it, as well as holding the desire to collaborate with others and develop workable social solutions. This acknowledgment of one of his Genius qualities was the necessary first step to establish it as an important part of his identity, and for him to give time to it in his daily life.

Having identified this Genius quality, Ryan began to see his household role in a different light. Instead of trying to find his life purpose solely through his self-expression as a husband and father, he realized that maintaining a household and caring for his family was *one* path of self-expression for him, while identifying with his Genius quality regarding social issues was another, and just as important to his life-purpose and fulfillment. His Genius had become something more real and corporeal for him, now that he could see one of the key areas to outwardly express it.

NEW LEARNING

When we can consciously feel the potential of our Genius within us, the task of expressing it becomes easier. Our work then is to make space for it as we move through our day and give it a place at the table of our identity. This means that we take the large idea or concept of Genius and personalize it to feel our own individual Genius in our present-moment awareness. We keep track of it, listen to it, and check in with it as a source of information, guidance, and direction. The more we tune in to our Genius daily, the more real it becomes to us.

One way to make your Genius more real is simply to name it when it shows up. For example, Ryan named his Genius quality "the Social Architect."

Parts theory is a well-known therapeutic model that sees humans' psychological selves as a collection of parts that make up our psychological identity. The reason this theory works so well is that it allows us to separate the different aspects of our behaviors and reactions into clearly defined parts that are identifiable, and therefore understandable.

For example, in your psychological collection of parts, you may have a three-year-old who is afraid of the sound of thunder, who can show up when it begins to storm. You may have a highly critical and negative part who finds faults in others as a way of self-protection. Perhaps there's a naïve part of you who wants to see the best in others so much that you allow your personal boundaries to be crossed. Regardless of what psychological parts you may identify, the idea is to name them and their corresponding feelings and behaviors so you have a frame of reference to work with them as they appear in your emotional awareness.

Similarly, naming your Genius and recognizing what it feels like when your Genius is present and functioning is a way of making it a part of your daily life. Even though our Genius is not an emotion or a part of our psychology, it is a part of our *larger innate identity*, and we feel a certain way when it is active and expressive. Consciously identifying and naming how it feels and what is being expressed when your Genius is activated will allow you to see how often your Genius is calling you to express its gifts—your unique work in the world.

Let's work with your primaconscious to mine some information about your Genius to help you to recognize and name it in your daily life.

GUIDED EXERCISE

(Listen to the audio version on www.thegeniusway.com/guidedexercises, or read one sentence at a time, then close your eyes and follow the visuals that arise.)

Allow yourself to feel the safety and security of the room you are sitting in now, where a safe and supportive container has been established for you to have a rich and rewarding inner experience related to your Genius qualities.

Feel your chair supporting your body, the floor of the building supporting your chair, and the very earth supporting the building you are in. This is the perfect place to be, and everything is set up to support and enhance your personal experience.

Allow yourself the freedom to drift back in time to a period of your life, at whatever physical age, when you were actually experiencing and expressing an aspect of your inborn Genius callings. This is a time or experience when you were feeling a sense of direction and purpose, using your talents, and being acknowledged for them.

What do you see yourself doing?

_____

_____

_____

_____

_____

_____

Take time to notice any thoughts, feelings, or impressions from this period that want to appear to you now, because they are important to your exploration.

Allow a few words to emerge that describe these thoughts, feelings, and impressions regarding your experience of expressing your Genius qualities. Write them down here.

_____

_____

_____

_____

Now allow yourself to become aware of something or someone that appeared in your life that distracted or inhibited this Genius expression. There may be a particular event or a gradual process, but somehow the priority of expressing your Genius became sidelined or lost.

You are able to see all of this without being emotionally triggered or sidetracked. You are able to simply witness everything with a sense of gentle curiosity and detachment. Take a few moments to explore this event or process. Take note of the people or circumstances involved.

As you witness this event or set of circumstances, see if you can discover the exact moment when you turned away from what your Genius was calling for you to express.

Write down your experience here.

_____

_____

_____

_____

_____

_____

_____

With this pivotal moment firmly established and held in your awareness, allow yourself to drift slowly forward in time, back to your present age. Still holding this pivotal moment in your present-time awareness, allow yourself to deliberately turn your attention back to your expression of your Genius quality.

It doesn't matter what that looks like or if it even makes sense to you in your present life situation. Just allow yourself the freedom to reconnect to that eternally present Genius quality that you have retrieved from your past.

This personal and special quality has a message for your present-day self.

What is this message?

_____

_____

_____

_____

_____

_____

_____

Allow the message that is expressed to you by your Genius to show you an example of how it wants to manifest in your present-day life. See a picture or image of yourself as you are now, expressing your Genius manifestation.

Without judgment or critique, just allow yourself to be surprised by what you see. Take note of this image by writing it down.

_____

_____

_____

_____

_____

_____

_____

With this experience solidly rooted in your present life, when you are ready, allow yourself to slowly bring your awareness back to your physical body, sitting in your chair in this room, and slowly open your eyes and be present.

INSIGHT PROTOCOL

Let's use the Genius Way Insight Protocol to curate your experience of naming your Genius when it appeared in your life.

IDENTIFY YOUR INSIGHT

From your content-mining experience, name an insight that occurred to you about one of your Genius qualities. Think about something that you understood about yourself in a new way or from a different perspective than your usual one.

_____

_____

_____

_____

_____

_____

_____

FIND YOUR INSIGHT IMAGE

Thinking about your experience, allow an image that represents your insight to come into focus in your mind's eye. What is the image that appears and represents this insight?

_____

_____

_____

_____

_____

_____

FIND THE SEED FEELING IN YOUR IMAGE

Holding the image of your insight in your mind's eye, allow a feeling to arise in your awareness concerning this image. What does this image make you feel? This is the seed feeling contained within your image.

_____

_____

_____

_____

_____

_____

_____

_____

COMMIT TO EXPRESSING SOMETHING FROM THE SEED FEELING

What do you want to express from your Genius as a response to your seed feeling? Identify something that you can express from your Genius insight and commit to taking an action.

I make a commitment to express my Genius self to:

_____

_____

_____

_____

_____

_____

_____

MAKE A SYMBOLIC EXPRESSION

Take a small symbolic action from your insight *right now* to start your momentum. What symbolic action do you make to acknowledge and represent your insight, image, seed feeling, and your commitment to expressing your Genius outwardly in the world?

_____

_____

_____

_____

_____

_____

_____

EXPRESS YOUR DOUBTS

Use this section to identify any doubts that are arising about your Genius process or your ability to express from your Genius. When we can identify our doubts, we can examine them for clarity and truthfulness.

_____

_____

_____

_____

_____

_____

_____

LIFE SKILL ONE AFFIRMATION

I have rediscovered an aspect of my Genius that I had forgotten about long ago. I am happy and excited to reconnect to the organic interest and spark that this quality holds for me. I am supported and empowered to take action from a place inside of me that is curious, open, engaged, and purposeful. I identify with my own Genius as an aspect of my core identity.

LIFE SKILL TWO —
Learning the Difference Between Your
Genius and Wound Drives

CHECK IN

After naming your Genius and identifying one of your Genius qualities in Life Skill One, let's add another life skill to your toolbox. Understanding what motivates your actions and self-expression is the key to ensuring that you're actually creating the best circumstances for a fulfilling life. In this chapter you'll learn about your Genius and Wound Drives, and how to tell the difference between them.

Use your unconditional positive self-regard as you move through the exercises. As you learn to let go of self-judgments during the learning process, your experience will be one of interest, curiosity, and discovery.

CLIENT STORY

Lisa was a client in her mid-thirties who struggled with obsessive/compulsive symptoms. This made it difficult to for her to trust herself enough to make life choices or to feel confident about the decisions she did make. At times even simple decisions were difficult for her, due to the pressure that she put herself under to make the "best" choice.

Lisa worked two jobs, each one serving to bring out an aspect of herself. As a designer, she loved creating innovative graphics and logos, and as a writer, she was able to present her opinions and ideas.

In our work together, we identified Lisa's childhood reaction to her parent's divorce as a likely cause of some of her obsessive issues, and along with them the habit of self-doubt that she developed at an early age as a survival behavior.

One of the complicating issues I could see was that Lisa wasn't able to discern the difference between her Wound and Genius Drives. She, like most of us, had both psychological woundings that required healing *and* specific Genius aspects that needed a path to outward expression.

To help Lisa to develop a better sense for how each drive feels in her life experience, we took one example of each drive as it showed up in her daily life and identified the feelings and qualities associated with each one to illustrate the differences.

In the case of her Wound Drive, Lisa was able to identify the feeling of never wanting to make a wrong decision so that others would always love and care for her. She also identified a need to develop a deeper trust that those in her life who loved her weren't going to leave. Conversely, from her Genius Drive, Lisa felt a sense of vitality and importance when she was designing a logo or branding materials for one of her clients, accessing her innate creativity and self-expression.

We spent some time in our sessions drawing clear distinctions between how each drive feels to her when it shows up in her life experience. Whether working as a designer, a writer, or in her personal life, an overweening need to please or anxiety that she would be negatively judged, and relief at being praised (not abandoned), signaled to her that her Wound Drive was engaged. A sense of newness and excitement when she was offering an elegant, beautiful, or clever design solution, written article, or useful service, and the absence of self-doubt told her that her Genius was at work. Knowing the different feelings at the base of each drive helped her to develop a better understanding of which drive she was using to make her daily life decisions, and how each drive motivates her actions toward a particular destination.

NEW LEARNING

Learning to recognize the difference between the motivation that comes from your Genius Drive or your Wound Drive is important because energetically, they have different goals. Your Wound Drive wants to heal, resolve, and return to the pre-wounded state. These are wonderful goals, and we might spend much of our life energy on them. It is essential work to heal from old wounds and traumas so we can live our lives in the present moment and move on to newer goals and dreams.

Separately, your Genius Drive primarily wants to express something in particular that you carry in your primaconscious DNA. This is a new expression, and it is not based on correcting something from the past that went wrong. As such, the motivation and direction of the Genius Drive isn't a returning, but more of a striking out towards the future, and one of experimentation and discovery. The Genius Drive is the part of ourselves in which existence's unique expression of us is encoded. The motivation contained within it comes from a deeper and older place than our personal psychology. It pertains directly to our individual life purpose.

So a key question to ask yourself, in order to see which drive your motivation is coming from, is: "Am I wanting a resolution or am I trying to explore something new with this action, decision, or expression?"

For example, whether in my role as a therapist or in my personal life, I tend to encourage people in their personal pursuits, support their creative ideas, and nurture their dreams and goals. Through my own personal psychological work, I've identified this quality as coming from my Wound Drive, since as a child I didn't feel encouraged in this way. In my expression of encouragement to others, I experience a feeling of wanting to heal, and of not wanting others to feel under-supported in their creativity, like I felt as a child. The *way* I am able to support others, however—my ability to connect with them and convey an idea or concept in a way that they can grasp and apply to their own lives—is one of my Genius qualities, and is motivated by my Genius Drive. This ability or gift has always been with me, and it feels wonderful and fulfilling to share it with others. When I look closely at how either of these motivations feels, they are unmistakably different.

Let's do an exercise to bring out the feeling of motivation from each of these drives.

GUIDED EXERCISE

(Listen to the audio version on www.thegeniusway.com/guidedexercises, or read one sentence at a time, then close your eyes and follow the visuals that arise.)

Allow yourself to feel the safety and security of the room you are sitting in now, where a safe and supportive container has been established for you to have a rich and rewarding inner experience related to your Genius qualities.

Feel your chair supporting your body, the floor of the building supporting your chair, and the very earth supporting the building you are in. This is the perfect place to be, and everything is set up to support and enhance your personal experience.

Imagine that you are walking through the woods by yourself. It is a lovely fall day, and you can see the afternoon sunlight filtering through the tree canopy above you, the leaves having turned to varying shades of red, orange, and gold. Every so often a leaf comes loose and gently glides to the ground.

As you make your way along the path, you witness something the size of a leaf falling from a tree onto the path ahead of you. As it nears the ground, you observe how it falls more quickly, observably heavier than a leaf. You walk up to the object to see what it is. On closer inspection, you discover that it is a baby bird who has fallen out of its nest. It is alive and healthy, but slightly stunned from the fall.

For a moment, exchange places and become this bird, and feel what it feels like to be in this predicament. Name the feeling or feelings of having fallen from your nest and suddenly landing here on the ground.

The feelings you are having as the bird represent something that wants to be healed in you, and therefore are feelings emanating from your Wound Drive. They are not good or bad, just a sense of wanting to return to a state of wholeness. Name one or more of those feelings.

_____

_____

_____

_____

_____

Now come back to yourself as the observer. Name your feelings as you consider how to respond to the bird's predicament.

_____

_____

_____

_____

_____

_____

_____

As you are deciding what, if any, action to take, the bird starts to move, slightly at first, and then suddenly opens its wings and flies back up to its nest in the tree.

Take a moment to observe your feelings about this new turn of events. Something happened that you hadn't foreseen, and you feel something about it.

Without the burden of having to fix, heal, or resolve anything, your feelings can turn to your personal insight about this experience, and are therefore representative of your Genius Drive.

Notice the difference between how you felt when experiencing something new and unexpected happening, and how you felt as you were trying to help the bird.

Take note of the difference of how it feels between your own Wound Drive and your Genius Drive.

_____

_____

_____

_____

_____

With this experience solidly rooted in your present life, when you are ready, allow yourself to slowly bring your awareness back to your physical body, sitting in your chair in this room, and slowly open your eyes and be present.

INSIGHT PROTOCOL

Follow the steps below to use the Genius Way Insight Protocol to curate your experience of differentiating between your Genius and Wound Drives.

IDENTIFY YOUR INSIGHT

From your guided visualization experience, name an insight from this guided experience about your Genius and Wound Drives. Think about something that you understood about yourself in a new way or from a different perspective than your usual one.

_____

_____

_____

_____

_____

_____

FIND YOUR INSIGHT IMAGE

Thinking about your insight, allow an image that represents your insight to come into focus in your mind's eye. What is the image that appears and represents this insight?

_____

_____

_____

_____

_____

FIND THE SEED FEELING IN YOUR IMAGE

Holding the image of your insight in your mind's eye, allow a feeling to arise in your awareness concerning this image. What does this image make you feel? This is the seed feeling contained within your image.

_____

_____

_____

_____

_____

_____

_____

COMMIT TO EXPRESSING SOMETHING FROM THE SEED FEELING

What do you want to express from your Genius as a response to your seed feeling? Identify something that you can express from your Genius insight and commit to taking an action.

I make a commitment to express my Genius self to:

_____

_____

_____

_____

_____

_____

MAKE A SYMBOLIC EXPRESSION

Take a small symbolic action from your insight *right now* to start your momentum. What symbolic action do you make to acknowledge and represent your insight, image, seed feeling, and your commitment to expressing your Genius outwardly in the world?

_____

_____

_____

_____

_____

_____

_____

EXPRESS YOUR DOUBTS

Use this section to identify any doubts that are arising about your Genius process or your ability to express from your Genius. When we can identify our doubts, we can examine them for clarity and truthfulness.

_____

_____

_____

_____

_____

_____

LIFE SKILL TWO AFFIRMATION

I have wounds to heal, and I also have gifts to share. I take responsibility for healing my own wounds and I take responsibility for expressing my Genius gifts with the world. Before my woundings, I have my Genius. Expressing my Genius is natural and necessary for me to live a fulfilling life.

LIFE SKILL THREE —
How to Identify Your Genius through Your Feeling Self

CHECK IN

Knowing how to discern the difference between your Genius and Wound Drives, as covered in the previous chapter, is a skill to practice and develop over time. Another skill that works hand-in-hand with that one is to identify your Genius through your feeling self. In this chapter you will learn to identify the *seed feelings* that show up when your individual Genius has been activated or is calling you to express something.

As you tune in to your inner senses to perceive these seed feelings, use your unconditional positive self-regard to allow whatever feelings you discover to exist without trying to change or modify them.

CLIENT STORY

Graham is a man in his mid-forties who requested Genius coaching because he was feeling a lack of meaning and purpose in his life, despite being a successful stockbroker. He had reached a career plateau, was feeling disinterested, and longed for a meaningful change. Unhappy in his marriage, Graham reported a lack of emotional connection with his wife, with whom he had tried for years to develop a deeper level of communication. But she had made it extremely clear that she wasn't open to trying couples therapy, didn't want to change, and liked their life as it was. Graham was currently having an extramarital affair. I could see his Genius expression and need for meaning and purpose striving to break out from the dull routine and disconnected life that had developed around him. The affair he was having was his unconscious attempt to try to create life movement.

Working with the Genius Way process, Graham was able to identify his Genius and the life movement he was trying to create by focusing on what he was *wanting to feel* in the future as a result of changing his life. When he looked closely, he saw that he longed to engage with life more fully and deeply by bringing his unexpressed intelligence and emotions into outward expression. For Graham, the key feeling that was driving his need for change was conscious engagement with others. He craved a sense of meaningful connection. He had tried for more than twenty years to feel these feelings by changing who his wife was, instead of opening an avenue of expression that would bring forth these feelings and Genius expressions for himself.

The life skill Graham was called to learn was to recognize the feeling of wanting to engage with life and others more fully and deeply, and to understand this feeling as a natural and valuable quality of his Genius self. His next step was to create an expression to bring about this feeling in his daily life. He joined several personal growth groups, where exploring self-expression and interpersonal connections was the stated goal. In this way he was able to directly act upon the seed feeling within his Genius that was calling him to connect with others in a meaningful way. This added the extra dimension to Graham's life that felt specifically fulfilling and purposeful for him by providing an avenue of expression for his Genius quality.

NEW LEARNING: IDENTIFYING FEELINGS ASSOCIATED WITH GENIUS

Our Genius speaks to us by allowing a feeling to surface as a way of pointing us in a particular direction, as if to say: "Do whatever you need to do to feel this feeling in your life." As mentioned earlier, I have named this type of feeling a *seed feeling*, since it is already present in us as an existential personal compass, direction, or orientation, and is not a product of or reaction to an outward stimulus. When you can sit quietly with the seed feelings beneath the images and ideas that arise as the dreams and hopes for your future, you can get a glimpse of your Genius and what will bring you a sense of purpose and fulfillment.

In Graham's case, the seed feeling was one of wanting meaningful engagement with others and a deeply felt need to express more of his intelligence and sensitivity in human connections. He began an affair with someone because he was trying to create this feeling of engagement in his outer life, wanting to express parts of himself that weren't being supported by his connection with his wife. Had he been able to see earlier that his sense of dissatisfaction wasn't because his wife wasn't good enough, but because he wasn't actively expressing his Genius, he might have accepted his wife as she was, or he might have ended his relationship simply because they had grown apart. Regardless, his feeling of wanting more engagement and connection in his life was a "feeling message" from his Genius that he now sensed with urgency.

If you look very closely at your inner world when you are envisioning something for your future, you'll find that you are actually wanting to feel something in particular. The vision, idea, or dream that arises is the symbol or image of the seed feeling that you want to have in the future. For example, the dream of the perfect partner, a better job or career, or a more desirable home or location is supported on a deeper inner level by a desire to *feel* a certain way. This seed feeling is part of your Genius DNA stored in your primaconscious, calling for an avenue of expression for one of your Genius qualities.

The seed feelings in our primaconscious may serve up images of our lives in the future as motivation to take action or as a psychic "prompt" to open a channel of expression for our Genius to appear in the world. Often, the form of expression our Genius wants to take may be quite different from how we have currently set up our lives—especially if we have only been following the wounded thread of our lives thus far. Regardless, tuning into your seed feelings is a key skill to practice as you are developing your Genius-based life.

GUIDED EXERCISE

(Listen to the audio version on www.thegeniusway.com/guidedexercises, or read one sentence at a time, then close your eyes and follow the visuals that arise.)

Allow yourself to feel the safety and security of the room you are sitting in now, where a safe and supportive container has been established for you to have a rich and rewarding inner experience related to your Genius qualities.

Feel your chair supporting your body, the floor of the building supporting your chair, and the very earth supporting the building you are in. This is the perfect place to be, and everything is set up to support and enhance your personal experience.

Imagine that you are sitting in your favorite chair. Your body feels relaxed, comfortable, and supported, and nothing is distracting you whatsoever.

Your heart and mind are free to explore the inner world you possess, and all of your attention and awareness can be placed there now.

Slowly you are becoming aware of an image of yourself in the future in which you are feeling fulfilled and purposeful. You are aware of the feeling of being exactly where you want to be and doing exactly what you want to do.

What do you see yourself doing?

_____

_____

_____

_____

_____

_____

What are the corresponding feelings that are happening simultaneously?

_____

_____

_____

_____

_____

Notice a few specific physical and emotional sensations that your experience is showing you.

For instance, if you are in the sun, feel its warmth on your face. If you are playing an instrument or singing, hear the tones and feel how they resonate with your body. If you are working at a new job, notice the environment and the people around you.

Find as many specific feelings and sensations as you can and name them here. In doing so, you are creating a space for this future expression of yourself to pull you towards it like a magnet.

_____

_____

_____

_____

_____

_____

Continue to notice all of the aspects of this experience that you can, and continue to name them as they arise in your consciousness.

_____

_____

_____

_____

_____

_____

As you are noticing and naming all of these things, something appears in the corner of your vision. Taking a look at this object, you see it is a calendar. What is the date on the calendar when this experience is happening? Say the date to yourself several times.

_____

_____

_____

_____

_____

_____

_____

Now you are getting ready to return to the present moment. Allow yourself to feel the vitality and reality of this experience in every cell of your body. You realize that this experience has already happened in a timeless place and is as real as anything else you have ever experienced. It is now a force or energy that is drawing you towards it as part of your life path.

Feeling secure in the awareness of this energy, you return to the present moment and space in this room, and when you're ready, you can open your eyes and be present.

INSIGHT PROTOCOL

Follow the steps below to use the Genius Way Insight Protocol to curate your experience of identifying your Genius qualities through your feeling self.

IDENTIFY YOUR INSIGHT

From your guided visualization experience, name an insight that occurred to you regarding the feelings connected to your Genius self and Genius qualities. Think about something that you understood about yourself in a new way or from a different perspective than your usual one.

_____

_____

_____

_____

_____

_____

FIND YOUR INSIGHT IMAGE

Thinking about your insight, allow an image that represents your insight to come into focus in your mind's eye. What is the image that appears and represents this insight?

_____

_____

_____

_____

_____

FIND THE SEED FEELING IN YOUR IMAGE

Holding the image of your insight in your mind's eye, allow a feeling to arise in your awareness concerning this image. What does this image make you feel? This is the *seed feeling* contained within your image.

_____

_____

_____

_____

_____

_____

_____

COMMIT TO EXPRESSING SOMETHING FROM THE SEED FEELING

What do you want to express from your Genius as a response to your seed feeling? Identify something that you can express from your Genius insight and commit to taking an action.

I make a commitment to express my Genius self to:

_____

_____

_____

_____

_____

_____

MAKE A SYMBOLIC EXPRESSION

Take a small symbolic action from your insight *right now* to start your momentum. What symbolic action do you make to acknowledge and represent your insight, image, seed feeling, and your commitment to expressing your Genius outwardly in the world?

_____

_____

_____

_____

_____

_____

_____

EXPRESS YOUR DOUBTS

Use this section to identify any doubts that are arising about your Genius process or your ability to express from your Genius. When we can identify our doubts, we can examine them for clarity and truthfulness.

_____

_____

_____

_____

_____

_____

_____

LIFE SKILL THREE AFFIRMATION

I recognize my Genius callings by how they feel to me. I trust that my seed feelings are here to guide me to living a fulfilling life through acknowledging my Genius self and qualities. I understand that I simply have to check in with how I feel to know if I am on my own Genius path that leads me to a personal sense of meaning and purpose.

LIFE SKILL FOUR —
How to Change: Where the Need to Change Comes From

CHECK IN

Now that you're on your way to making your Genius a consistent presence in your life by practicing the first three Genius Way life skills, let's learn a foundational skill that identifies the mechanics of how to make a lasting life change. In this chapter we'll demystify our seeming inability to change our lives by looking at what we *can* actually change.

As you tune in to your inner senses to perceive these seed feelings,
Make the effort to apply your unconditional positive self-regard to
anything you uncover during the Genius Way process. This will enable
you to hold enough inner space for this new part of you
to begin to grow.

CLIENT STORY

Every client begins therapy because of a desire to change something in their life, and Calvin was no exception. He had experienced a significant amount of childhood trauma and had spent much of his life expressing from his Wound Drive in his relationships and social settings. Often he would be attracted to abusive people, unconsciously calling them into his life as a way of trying to heal his childhood trauma, only to be abused and traumatized again.

Calvin was naturally intelligent and insightful, but the expression of his intelligence was often overshadowed by his emotional dysregulation and social anxiety.

After several sessions, we discovered that one aspect of his desire to change his life was coming from his unexpressed Genius quality as a teacher, which was calling for him to create an avenue of expression for it. Calvin was also feeling a deep calling to express his curiosities and interests about cultural diversity issues, and to use his intelligence and leadership qualities in a purposeful way. When he spoke about this topic, Calvin became alert and energized, inspired and erudite. He felt enlivened and substantial, with no sign of hesitancy in his expression, and no sign of his trauma.

We worked together to help Calvin accept the period of his life when he had been traumatized as *one* part of himself that needed to be acknowledged and cared for. Through some key psychological interventions in therapy, Calvin was able to actively address this wounded part when it showed up. But to facilitate the lasting change that he was craving, Calvin also needed to create an avenue of expression for his Genius qualities—leadership skills and a passion for the topic of cultural diversity—that were being neglected and unexpressed. He began to participate in a local group that promoted diversity and social justice, where he could openly express these two Genius qualities and demonstrate this aspect of his identity to himself and others. This new and targeted expression eventually led him to enroll in a graduate program in cultural diversity that enlivened his natural interests and curiosities, and helped him to further develop his personal vision and expression. By creating an avenue of expression for his Genius, he expanded his sense of identity to now include both his Wound and Genius Drives.

Acknowledging the feeling and urgency for change as a call from his Genius was the medicine Calvin needed to see his life from a different perspective and begin to create the change he was longing for. By aligning the change he was wanting to make with his existing Genius callings, Calvin could now make a change that could stick. Because his Genius already wanted to express itself in this way, he was now working in concert with something innate and organic in him. He therefore had the full energy of his Genius Drive to fuel the change and make it a healthy and vibrant lifelong expression.

NEW LEARNING: HOW CAN WE CHANGE?

In a Genius-based framework, we create lasting change by coming more into alignment with our inborn Genius qualities and expression. We recognize that feeling the need for change is a calling to become more in harmony with our individual nature, and with our Genius qualities that have been there since birth.

In psychological terms, and particularly from a psychodynamic lens, change begins first by making unconscious psychic material conscious. By doing so, the psychic energy contained in the unconscious material becomes available to our conscious self, and we can now use the released unconscious energy to produce forward life movement due to the shift in our perspective. Another way to describe this shift in perspective is that we gain or have an insight or personal realization about our life.

In a Genius-based life approach, instead of making unconscious psychic material conscious, we make some of our *primaconscious* material conscious. That is to say, we bring our Genius qualities to our conscious awareness. This revelation shifts our perspective as well, but the insight is gained from seeing our latent Genius qualities, as opposed to seeing the source and secret of our woundings. The energy released into conscious awareness from this type of shift in perspective is generative and expressive, as opposed to restorative and healing. When we can consciously see our inherent Genius aspects, we become energized and motivated to create and express something new.

To make conscious life changes that are aligned with our individual Genius qualities, we first need to identify one or more of those qualities, and then create an avenue of expression for it in our life. The identification and the active expression are equally important.

Let's do this exercise to discover one of the Genius qualities in your primaconscious and create a way for you to express it.

GUIDED EXERCISE

(Listen to the audio version on www.thegeniusway.com/guidedexercises, or read one sentence at a time, then close your eyes and follow the visuals that arise.)

Allow yourself to feel the safety and security of the room you are sitting in now, where a safe and supportive container has been established for you to have a rich and rewarding inner experience related to your Genius qualities.

Feel your chair supporting your body, the floor of the building supporting your chair, and the very earth supporting the building you are in. This is the perfect place to be, and everything is set up to support and enhance your personal experience.

Imagine that you are sitting in your living room at home with your eyes closed and asking your primaconscious to share some of its content to help you change something about your life.

As you are silently waiting for your primaconscious to respond to you, instead of receiving an insight, you feel compelled to get up and walk over to a specific spot in your living room that is calling for your attention.

You move towards the spot and surprisingly see a trap door in your floor that you hadn't noticed before. You open it.

In the space under your floor, you see an extremely valuable object that belongs to you that you had somehow forgotten about.

What is this object?

_____

_____

_____

_____

_____

_____

Allow this object to speak or convey a message about its importance to you.

What does it communicate to you?

_____

_____

_____

_____

_____

_____

Bring this object up into your living room so it can be part of your everyday life.

As you look around to see where you want to place this object in your living room, you notice that there isn't an adequate space for it, and that you have to rearrange your living room to allow the object to fit.

What do you have to move or rearrange to allow this object to have a proper, permanent place that illustrates its importance to you?

_____

_____

_____

_____

_____

_____

How does it feel to prioritize this valuable object over the other items in your living space?

_____

_____

_____

_____

_____

This object represents one of your Genius qualities. It is now a living presence in your life because you've given it a prioritized place in your conscious world.

With this experience solidly rooted in your present life, when you are ready, allow yourself to slowly bring your awareness back to your physical body, sitting in your chair in this room, and slowly open your eyes and be present.

INSIGHT PROTOCOL

Follow the steps below to use the Genius Way Insight Protocol to curate your experience of what you're wanting to change in your life.

IDENTIFY YOUR INSIGHT

From your guided visualization experience, name an insight that occurred to you about something you want to change in your life. Think about something that you understood about yourself in a new way or from a different perspective than your usual one.

_____

_____

_____

_____

_____

_____

_____

FIND YOUR INSIGHT IMAGE

Thinking about your insight, allow an image that represents your insight to come into focus in your mind's eye. What is the image that appears and represents this insight?

_____

_____

_____

_____

_____

_____

FIND THE SEED FEELING IN YOUR IMAGE

Holding the image of your insight in your mind's eye, allow a feeling to arise in your awareness concerning this image. What does this image make you feel? This is the seed feeling contained within your image.

_____

_____

_____

_____

_____

_____

COMMIT TO EXPRESSING SOMETHING FROM THE SEED FEELING

What do you want to express from your Genius as a response to your seed feeling? Identify something that you can express from your Genius insight and commit to taking an action.

I make a commitment to express my Genius self to:

_____

_____

_____

_____

_____

_____

MAKE A SYMBOLIC EXPRESSION

Take a small symbolic action from your insight *right now* to start your momentum. What symbolic action do you make to acknowledge and represent your insight, image, seed feeling, and your commitment to expressing your Genius outwardly in the world?

_____

_____

_____

_____

_____

_____

_____

EXPRESS YOUR DOUBTS

Use this section to identify any doubts that are arising about your Genius process, or your ability to express from your Genius. When we can identify our doubts, we can examine them for clarity and truthfulness.

_____

_____

_____

_____

_____

_____

_____

LIFE SKILL FOUR AFFIRMATION

I am empowered to change anything in my life that restricts my ability to live as my Genius self. When I align myself with my innate Genius qualities, I am able to easily change any habits or patterns I have developed, regardless of how long I have been practicing them.

LIFE SKILL FIVE —
How to Break Habits:
Changing the Momentum

CHECK IN

Now that you understand where the healthy desire to change comes from, you need a life skill that works with the mechanics of change. In this chapter you'll learn how to break old habits that have been set up unconsciously in your past. By actively setting up a new and conscious habit that is a continuation of your Genius expression, you'll create new momentum that will change your life direction.

Even though it may seem challenging to change old habits, building on your ability to exercise unconditional positive self-regard will allow you to release any self-judgment and make room in your awareness for the changes to take root and build momentum.

CLIENT STORY

Leslie was a working single mom who came to my office with symptoms of anxiety. She described her main problem as a self-worth issue that translated into having poor boundaries with other people, especially around how she valued herself in work and personal settings. We soon identified Leslie's habit of overextending herself in work and personal relationships to the point where she had no time or energy left for her own projects and ideas. Her habit was one of trying to attain a sense of life purpose from garnering others' approval.

As Leslie worked on her anxiety and personal boundary issues, she opened up about her interest in creating learning content for children. As she was speaking, she showed an intellectual sharpness and an ability to see into her situation with great insight. I saw the telltale signs of someone in touch with their Genius qualities in how she became empowered and enlivened about these interests.

While Leslie was expressing this aspect of herself in our sessions, I noticed that her anxious symptomology had disappeared. I pointed this out to her, and consequently she observed an important truth: that she could not hold the identification with her anxiety *and* express her Genius at the same time. This illustrated to me that one of the natural gifts contained in her primaconscious was being suppressed while she was identified with her anxiety; and if she could develop an ongoing awareness of her Genius Drive as an alternative aspect of herself to identify with, she could gain a healthier personal perspective and change the momentum around her self-worth and personal boundary issues. I worked with Leslie to consciously acknowledge her intellectual sharpness and clarity as a quality of her Genius, and to create a statement to remind herself of that. Leslie came up with the phrase "I protect my time and ideas because they are important."

Leslie had a work colleague, Isaac, a co-manager who would overload Leslie's schedule with extra work that Isaac should have been doing himself. Typically instead of standing up for herself and holding a strong personal boundary around her work schedule, Leslie would take on the extra work to "people please" and to be seen as a team player others could count on to solve problems. She would always feel an accompanying collapse into self-doubt, as her habitual motivation to act was based on her Wound Drive—her unconscious attempt to heal a wounded aspect of her past.

To change this dynamic for Leslie, we created a new habit to practice that used Leslie's Genius Drive as a base of motivation. Now, whenever Isaac attempted to bully her, and she felt the feeling of collapsing into self-doubt, it was Leslie's cue to recall her Genius phrase, "I protect my time and ideas because they are important." This became her touchstone to identify with her Genius qualities as a creative person with vision and direction, and her self-reminder allowed her to refuse Isaac's requests. She began practicing this new habit of acknowledging her Genius self and her Genius qualities as an alternate part of her genuine identity. Practicing this identification over and over again changed her habitual momentum, prevented her from falling into her old, unhealthy habit, and allowed her to express her Genius self outwardly in the world.

Eventually, Leslie was able to more fully incorporate her Genius as part of her current identity. She developed a website where she published learning videos for children and directed a small team that helped to manifest her creative vision. As she continued to practice her new habit, a number of old and unbalanced relationships fell away, and she was able to create many new work and social relationships that supported her newly established healthy personal boundaries.

NEW LEARNING: THE MOMENTUM OF HABITS

Regarding the making and breaking of habits, we have to be aware of the difference between energy and momentum. In this case, energy is the raw material that we use to create momentum by repeating the same action over and over again.

In my childhood, my friends and I would create a "whirlpool" in the water in my aboveground pool by circling the inside edge of the pool. We would "lend" our energy to the water, walking in the same direction until our energy translated into momentum, and the water would then carry us along by itself. The momentum we created had been stored and was now visible as moving water, giving us the illusion that the moving water had its own energy.

The fact that we are always "lending" our energy is the key here. We can't *not* lend our energy to something. We just have to realize that we can choose what we're energizing. Remember that, just as we spend our time, we are spending our daily energy on some thought or action. We have an allowance of energy that *is* going to be spent today. We are the stewards of this energy. To break a habit, we need to understand that the daily energy we have is ours to spend in any way we choose. Any significant change will come by seeing what we are actually choosing to spend our energy on.

Leslie, for example, found that once she began to direct her energy into developing her new project, it took on a life of its own—it gained momentum in her life. She found ideas for it would come to her spontaneously throughout her day, and she looked forward to working on it each evening.

The energy of a habit, which has its foundation in either our Genius or Wound Drive, only has the energy that we have lent it. The habit will expend that borrowed energy as momentum. If it no longer has access to the source, and because it has no energy of its own, it will slow down and eventually stop. Remember that the foundational energy of a habit, healthy or not, will drive and point us to a particular outcome and goal. Our Wound Drive points us towards healing and resolution, and our Genius Drive moves us toward generativity and new expression.

The first thing to realize is that we are the dispensers of this energy, and that the power of our habits doesn't come from anywhere else. We just aren't familiar with the part of ourselves that is the bestower of energies. Once we realize that the habit itself has no power, the dynamic of the problem changes and is less of a challenge.

Our job as the habit-breaker is to stop lending our psychic energy to the momentum of the old habit, and instead allow it to dissipate over time. This effort can't be done directly. As an indirect effort, it is the focusing on a different habit, and lending our energy to the new activity, that indirectly allows the old momentum to dissipate.

Again, think of the "whirlpool" in a small pool, but now we are walking against the momentum of the water. For a while it feels as if we weigh a thousand pounds as we practice our new habit. Instead of feeling the vitality of practicing something new, we may only feel the drag of moving against our old momentum. But after a while of lending our energy to another pursuit, the original habit and momentum loses all of its borrowed power and ceases to be a problem for us.

Using the Genius Way process to create a new habit, we first identify an interest that is connected to our Genius Drive and then develop a consistent way to experiment and practice with it. Again, this draws our energy away from our old habit and invests it into our healthy and more directed one.

Feeding an old habit with our daily energy is a choice, however difficult it may be to come to grips with that fact. It can feel as if our old habits are so strong that we are somehow powerless over them. In reality, our habits only live on the power or energy that we have given them. And each time we empower our old habits, somewhere inside of us, in a small moment, we are making the choice to do so. Once we can see the actual moment of making the choice to feed an old habit, we can also see how to make a different choice; and thereby we can make a change in our lives.

Using this guided journey, let's ask your primaconscious to show you one of your Genius qualities to practice in place of an old habit.

GUIDED EXERCISE

(Listen to the audio version on www.thegeniusway.com/guidedexercises, or read one sentence at a time, then close your eyes and follow the visuals that arise.)

Allow yourself to feel the safety and security of the room you are sitting in now, where a safe and supportive container has been established for you to have a rich and rewarding inner experience related to your Genius qualities.

Feel your chair supporting your body, the floor of the building supporting your chair, and the very earth supporting the building you are in. This is the perfect place to be, and everything is set up to support and enhance your personal experience.

Take a moment to identify an old habit that you'd like to break or change.

_____

_____

_____

_____

_____

_____

_____

See this habit as a stream flowing downhill, with a well-worn bed that guides the water's course and trajectory consistently over time.

Currently, your stream/habit's water flows into a ditch and disappears from view.

Alongside this ditch, you have created a garden with plants that you've chosen to grow. You notice that the garden is dry, and the plants are small and wilted from a lack of water. You would like to direct your stream to this garden as a new habit.

Now see yourself walking upstream along this stream/habit, all the way up the mountain to its source.

Eventually you find the beginning of this habit/stream as small spring that emerges from the ground at the top. Take a moment to see how small and gentle it is as it emerges.

You can see that as it begins to flow downwards, gaining momentum, whatever it encounters guides and changes its course.

You see that a rock in the path of its flow guides the water to one side, down the mountain, eventually into the ditch.

There is a word or phrase engraved on this rock, representing your old habit. What is this word or phrase?

_____

_____

_____

_____

_____

_____

You can see that at this point, you have the capability of changing the direction of your habit/stream very easily.

Before the flow of the stream reaches your old habit/rock, place a different rock in the path of your small stream to make it flow instead to the other side, in the direction of your garden.

Write a word or phrase on this rock to represent the new habit you will be practicing. What do you write here?

_____

_____

_____

_____

How does it feel to make this small change?

_____

_____

_____

_____

_____

_____

_____

Now your stream/habit is taking a different course. Begin to walk alongside it down the mountain as it makes its way to your garden.

Look to the side where the old streambed is now dry and empty, as it is no longer needed and as the flow of your stream/habit moves in the direction you've consciously chosen.

See how it effortlessly moves down a new path, arriving and irrigating your garden, bringing precious life-giving energy to the things you've chosen to grow.

By making a small change at the moment of choice, you have made a large change in the overall quality and direction of your life.

With this experience solidly rooted in your present life, when you are ready, allow yourself to slowly bring your awareness back to your physical body, sitting in your chair in this room, and slowly open your eyes and be present.

INSIGHT PROTOCOL

Follow the steps below to use the Genius Way Insight Protocol to curate your experience of changing the momentum of a habit.

IDENTIFY YOUR INSIGHT

From your guided visualization experience, name an insight that occurred to you about breaking a habit and creating a new momentum. Think about something that you understood about yourself in a new way or from a different perspective than your usual one.

_____

_____

_____

_____

_____

_____

FIND YOUR INSIGHT IMAGE

Thinking about your insight, allow an image that represents your insight to come into focus in your mind's eye. What is the image that appears and represents this insight?

_____

_____

_____

_____

_____

_____

FIND THE SEED FEELING IN YOUR IMAGE

Holding the image of your insight in your mind's eye, allow a feeling to arise in your awareness concerning this image. What does this image make you feel? This is the seed feeling contained within your image.

_____

_____

_____

_____

_____

_____

_____

COMMIT TO EXPRESSING SOMETHING FROM THE SEED FEELING

What do you want to express from your Genius as a response to your seed feeling? Identify something that you can express from your Genius insight and commit to taking an action.

I make a commitment to express my Genius self to:

_____

_____

_____

_____

_____

_____

MAKE A SYMBOLIC EXPRESSION

Take a small symbolic action from your insight *right now* to start your momentum. What symbolic action do you make to acknowledge and represent your insight, image, seed feeling, and your commitment to expressing your Genius outwardly in the world?

_____

_____

_____

_____

_____

_____

_____

_____

EXPRESS YOUR DOUBTS

Use this section to identify any doubts that are arising about your Genius process, or your ability to express from your Genius. When we can identify our doubts, we can examine them for clarity and truthfulness.

_____

_____

_____

_____

_____

_____

_____

LIFE SKILL FIVE AFFIRMATION

When I recognize a habit that I want to break, I can consciously remove my energy from it by creating a new conscious habit with its own momentum. When I create a new habit that is congruous with my Genius, I have the support of creative existence in making that life change..

LIFE SKILL SIX —
The Time Dilemma—How to Prioritize the Way You Spend Your Time

CHECK IN

As you practice creating a new conscious habit, it will continue to gain momentum and soon will be carrying your life experience along with it. Let's reinforce this momentum by taking a closer look at time. In this chapter, we'll take a deep dive into how you are currently using your time each day, and how to make the changes needed to use your time in a way that actually benefits you and your Genius expression.

Be sure to use unconditional positive self-regard as you move through the chapter. Affirm that it's possible for you to use your time to express your Genius qualities throughout your day.

CLIENT STORY

Wayne was in his early thirties and was seeking treatment for depression. He was also struggling with finding a life direction that felt meaningful and fulfilling. He was a very creative and active person with many skills and interests, all of which seemed equally important to him. We identified this as one of his primary issues: he was engaging in "magical time," or the idea that there was an unlimited amount of time every day to express all of his interests. When, at the end of each day, he didn't get to accomplish everything he wanted to, he became frustrated, deflated, self-judging, and disappointed in himself. Consequently, achieving his goals and dreams was put off until another day, and he was left feeling stuck in the rut of his routine, unable to move forward.

I recognized Wayne's inability to prioritize his daily expressions as his unconscious and ineffective habit. By disregarding the actual number of hours in a day and how he spent them, he was giving each of his ideas and passions an indefinite amount of his time, and he inevitably felt stymied and frustrated when his daily time allotment ran out.

Wayne had not yet understood that we develop our identities as we prioritize what we spend our time on; we become the individual we are, not only by what we choose to spend our time on, but also by the things we *don't* choose to do.

Wayne was, among many other things, a teacher and mentor. Using the Genius Way process, he was able to identify how his Genius was activated while he was teaching by recognizing how invigorated and alive he felt while he was doing it. By learning to perceive the difference between feelings associated with his Genius and the feelings of general curiosity and interest, he began to prioritize and assign actual time to his Genius expressions before his lesser interests.

Wayne loved to garden. He lived on a property that had plants to care for or to harvest year-round. He could easily spend all of his time maintaining them. To address the time issue, Wayne decided to consciously prioritize his Genius quality of mentoring students over his love of maintaining a garden. This meant that he consciously would allow his garden to become a bit overgrown and less tended to, and instead use more of his time to teach gardening to children at a local school. This way, Wayne was actively prioritizing his Genius callings over his lesser curiosities and interests by devoting the actual time that he had to spend to teaching. Using his time in this way allowed him to focus on his Genius quality of being a mentor and move forward with his life goals in a purposive way.

NEW LEARNING: TIME AS CURRENCY

Each one of us is born wealthy.

We don't all come into this world with money, possessions, and status, but certainly we are wealthy in terms of possibility. This wealth of possibility rests on two things: time and Genius.

Time

It's a simple truth that there is only one way to genuinely express what is important to us, and that is to spend our time doing it.

We will each have only a certain amount of time to spend on our life expression, and no one knows how much time they've been given. We can look at our time as our life currency.

Each day we are allotted a limited amount of this time currency to invest or squander. Since we can't stop time from moving into the future or save it for another day, we have no choice but to spend it today. Now. We do, however, have a choice about what to spend it on. And what we trade our time for creates our life experience.

Genius

Our personal Genius is also a source of wealth, because as far as we know, the universe has created each one of us only once, just as we are. Once we live out our life and spend the time we've been given, the particular human expression that we call ourself will never appear on the earth again.

Attuning to our innate Genius is the key to spending our time creatively and effectively; we must allow ourselves to actually inhabit the form and possibility we've been born as. An essential element then, to living a meaningful life, is to discover your inborn Genius callings and then *spend your time* expressing what you have found.

This means that unless we make a change in the status quo of how we're currently spending our time, or life currency, our Genius qualities and therefore our sense of life purpose will unsurprisingly continue to go unfelt and unexpressed. When we feel the proddings of our Genius, we must respectfully, even joyfully, answer the call.

You may find that even though you intend to make time to express your Genius every day, the intention doesn't manifest into an action. This is a dilemma that many people experience and is the very thing that stagnates and stifles our authentic Genius expression.

To begin this process, you must first take a hard look at how you are currently spending your time, to see how you are actually using this precious commodity.

For example, right now, put down this book and do a mental inventory of what you've spent your time currency on in the last twenty-four hours. Make a list or chart. You'll probably find that you spent around seven to eight hours sleeping; another twelve to fourteen hours eating, traveling, working, and meeting family obligations, and possibly exercising; and the last two to five hours were taken up by unexpected events and/or relaxing.

If this is the case, I think you can see where I'm going with this.

Even though you may have intended to spend some of your time on expressing your Genius, the intention didn't turn into an action.

Let's use a simple tool to make a bridge from intention to action. I'll ask you two *Action Questions* that are designed to help you to examine different aspects of your life so you can begin to make positive changes and create movement in your life experience.

ACTION QUESTIONS:

1. If you had to, where could you find and reallocate thirty minutes in your day to experiment with expressing your Genius callings?

_____

_____

_____

_____

2. When will you commit to begin?

_____

_____

_____

Answering these two simple questions places the responsibility of finding your life purpose squarely on your shoulders, *in time and space*. If you are being honest with yourself, you will have to take an action.

Taking this brief look at how you are spending your time currency sheds light on why your life may not be what you want it to be. Throughout the book, we'll be using a closer, deliberate investigation into the major areas of your life that will yield some essential information about what it will take for you in particular to feel purposeful and fulfilled.

In Walt Whitman's poem "Oh Me! Oh Life!" he poses a question to existence, asking what good comes from putting in the human effort of searching for individual purpose and expression. An answer came back to him:

> *That you are here—that life exists and identity,*
>
> *That the powerful play goes on, and you may contribute a verse.*
>
> —Walt Whitman

Time and Genius are indeed wealth, because without them, we couldn't assume the awesome responsibility of fully expressing who we are as individuals, and consequently add to the collective expression of our world by our participation.

Countless people throughout history have endeavored to ask and answer this exact question concerning what good comes from our efforts to express our individuality, and they had to recognize and then trade their wealth—*time* and *Genius*—to embody and become their own answer to this existential question.

GUIDED EXERCISE

(Listen to the audio version on www.thegeniusway.com/guidedexercises, or read one sentence at a time, then close your eyes and follow the visuals that arise.)

Allow yourself to feel the safety and security of the room you are sitting in now, where a safe and supportive container has been established for you to have a rich and rewarding inner experience related to your Genius qualities.

Feel your chair supporting your body, the floor of the building supporting your chair, and the very earth supporting the building you are in. This is the perfect place to be, and everything is set up to support and enhance your personal experience.

Imagine that you are living on your very own very small planet.

Take a moment to look around at this small world that you call your home.

Notice all of the sights, sounds, smells, and feelings that exist on your personal planet, and become aware of your experience of living here.

What is your daily routine in this world?

_____

_____

_____

_____

_____

_____

What do you spend your time doing?

_____

_____

_____

_____

_____

_____

_____

Take a moment to notice that whatever you spend your time on becomes stronger, more substantial, and more real.

As you walk your personal world, you become aware of a specific problem that is unique to your planet. You realize that without your intervention, this problem can eventually damage or even destroy your tiny world.

What is this problem that you have discovered that needs to be addressed?

_____

_____

_____

_____

_____

_____

_____

_____

_____

_____

Since it is up to you to come up with a solution to this problem, you ask the inner wisdom of your Genius spirit to provide an image or symbol that represents this solution.

You close your eyes and open yourself to the response from your Genius spirit.

It is important to allow whatever wants to be expressed to emerge from the depths of being where your Genius spirit exists. Take care not to judge, criticize, or change the answer that is provided to you.

What is the image or symbol that is presented to you?

_____

_____

_____

_____

How do you feel about this image or symbol?

_____

_____

_____

_____

_____

_____

Is there anything else that occurs to you in addition to what you've seen in your vision?

_____

_____

_____

_____

_____

_____

Now take a look around at your small world one more time.

What, if anything, has changed in your awareness about what you do with your time here?

_____

_____

_____

_____

_____

_____

_____

_____

See yourself spending time to address the issue with your planet with what you've uncovered in your vision.

Notice if anything looks or feels different now that you are spending time practicing the actions that will fix and heal your planet.

With this experience solidly rooted in your present life, when you are ready, allow yourself to slowly bring your awareness back to your physical body, sitting in your chair in this room, and slowly open your eyes and be present.

INSIGHT PROTOCOL

Follow the steps below to use the Genius Way Insight Protocol to curate your experience of how you are currently spending your time, and how you want to spend your time in the future.

IDENTIFY YOUR INSIGHT

From your guided visualization experience, name an insight that occurred to you about how you currently spend your time, or how you would like to spend your time. Think about something that you understood about yourself in a new way or from a different perspective than your usual one.

_____

_____

_____

_____

_____

_____

_____

_____

FIND YOUR INSIGHT IMAGE

Thinking about your insight, allow an image that represents your insight to come into focus in your mind's eye. What is the image that appears and represents this insight?

_____

_____

_____

_____

_____

_____

_____

FIND THE SEED FEELING IN YOUR IMAGE

Holding the image of your insight in your mind's eye, allow a feeling to arise in your awareness concerning this image. What does this image make you feel? This is the seed feeling contained within your image.

_____

_____

_____

_____

_____

_____

_____

COMMIT TO EXPRESSING SOMETHING FROM THE SEED FEELING

What do you want to express from your Genius as a response to your seed feeling? Identify something that you can express from your Genius insight and commit to taking an action.

I make a commitment to express my Genius self to:

_____

_____

_____

_____

MAKE A SYMBOLIC EXPRESSION

Take a small symbolic action from your insight *right now* to start your momentum. What symbolic action do you make to acknowledge and represent your insight, image, seed feeling, and your commitment to expressing your Genius outwardly in the world?

_____

_____

_____

_____

_____

_____

_____

_____

EXPRESS YOUR DOUBTS

Use this section to identify any doubts that are arising about your Genius process, or your ability to express from your Genius. When we can identify our doubts, we can examine them for clarity and truthfulness.

_____

_____

_____

_____

_____

_____

_____

LIFE SKILL SIX AFFIRMATION

I see time as a precious and limited commodity to use wisely. I prioritize my Genius expression in how I use my time because it provides me a sense of fulfillment. I use my time to express my Genius as the further expression of existence's expression of me.

LIFE SKILL SEVEN —
Connected vs. Disconnected Individualism:
Understanding the Difference

CHECK IN

In the last chapter, you took a close look at how you are spending your daily allotment of time, and how that choice affects the outcome of your life path and experience. Next, we'll consider the idea of individualism in terms of how it relates to existence itself. In this chapter you'll learn how to discover your connected individualism, and learn about yourself as a continuation of existence's original expression of you.

Unconditional positive self-regard is essential when we endeavor to experience ourselves as connected to existence. Remember that like anything we're trying to learn, unconditional positive self-regard needs to be practiced over time. Don't worry if it feels difficult at first. It gets easier the more you do it.

CLIENT STORY

Ellen was in her mid-sixties and came to see me to work on life transition issues. She had recently retired and was now facing the existential questions that she hadn't addressed while she was busy working and raising her family. Ellen had always been a seeker of truth and knowledge, and conscientiously explored various faiths and religions in an attempt to arrive at a "ground" of understanding about the universe and her place in it. For all of her searching and sincerity, the feeling of being at peace with her circumstances had eluded her.

After several sessions, we discovered that Ellen wasn't using her personal connection to existence as a way of moving consciously into the next phase of her life. Her current sense of self and self-expression was based on a *disconnected* individualism, or the feeling and core belief that there was nothing organically connecting her directly to existence and Creation.

One significant aspect of Ellen's life that affected her deeply was her anxiety about the wellbeing of her family members, to the point that she made their problems and challenges her own. In an excess of concern, she would carry their issues over into her own life, along with the stress and responsibility of needing to "fix" their situations for them. Not surprisingly, this habit eventually led to Ellen experiencing insomnia, anxiety, and panic attacks.

Ellen had no problem intellectually accepting the idea that she indeed had a Genius that holds her existential connectedness. But beyond this, she needed to *feel* that connection. I helped Ellen to mine her primaconscious for her particular Genius callings and qualities that transcended the thoughts or ideas she was holding about herself. As we progressed through the Genius Way process, Ellen discovered that sometimes her need to "fix" things was a manifestation of her need to feel in control—a desperate feeling she was able to identify as emanating from her Wound Drive, dating from a childhood loss. But she also discovered, as she explored her primaconscious, a strong and foundational reverence for all living things. This respect for and desire to nurture and protect people, animals, and nature had been there her entire life. And she felt it strongly as a positive energy, free of fear or anxiety.

The discovery of a deeper layer of herself allowed Ellen a way of connecting to existence through *sensing and feeling* what she already possessed in her original identity—a gift for nurturance and helping others to grow, her Genius qualities—instead of *thinking* about what was missing in her life experience and struggling to attain it, or fretting about others' problems.

Ellen was able to use this elemental connection as a way of changing how she related to her family members and their circumstances. Instead of anxiously taking on their difficulties, she was able to feel her Genius quality of care for others as her existential inheritance. Using this connectedness, she was able to see the difference between what she could actually do for her family members, and what was theirs to do for themselves. Ellen's awakened sense of connected individualism was the key to consciously respond rather than anxiously react to the people and situations in her life.

NEW LEARNING

Humans are living paradoxes in that we are at once a continuation of an expression of the universe and are simultaneously free to express ourselves as individuals. Our daily choice is either to consciously co-create with the intelligent universe as a connected individual or to try to do it on our own, disconnected from whatever created us.

This puts us in a peculiar position.

It means that we're free to choose whether to use our connection to the consciousness that created us as the foundation of our identity, or to use our disconnected individualism as such. What we do with this choice makes all the difference when it comes to living a Genius-based life.

I find it mystifying that we are all given the power of expression and creation, but—at least in our modern-day Western culture—we aren't taught how to use it. It seems that part of the great "fierce energy" experiment for most of humankind is that without being told, we've been tasked as individuals with figuring out how to wield this creative power on the fly. We have to learn as we go.

We aren't forced to use our connection to Creator or existence; we have a choice. When an individual does choose to use their connection, all of the energy stored in the drive of the original expression that we are—our Genius Drive—becomes available to us.

Conversely, to live as a disconnected individual is to not use our connection to the universe as our platform of identity. In this case we look to others' lives, comparing and judging ourselves to see how we measure up. Our basis for success or achievement rests solely on the feedback we receive from outside of ourselves, and not on how it feels for us, or how aligned we feel with our Genius.

A connected individual understands their basic connection to the creative universe, and the importance of living out the individualistic nature of themselves *as a piece of Creation*. There is a responsibility handed down from Creator to Creation—a responsibility for us to take on the mantle of creator ourselves. The task is to create and live an individual life that by design will never be repeated or created by anyone else, ever, throughout all of time. This realization is to see the opportunity of this individual life—*your* individual life—as the creation of a one-of-a-kind experience, expression, and gift to the world by continuing the original act of Creation.

Remember that the initial act of our being created also includes our being given, as individuals, the power of creation. We can see it in the thoughts we entertain every day in our minds. We are constantly creating. The Genius Way is about consciously using our inherited creative power to create something responsibly. It is to understand the great creative power we all possess, and about how we use that creative power to express ourselves in the world and to others.

Let's do an exercise that can help you to apply this idea to your own life.

GUIDED EXERCISE

(Listen to the audio version on www.thegeniusway.com/guidedexercises, or read one sentence at a time, then close your eyes and follow the visuals that arise.)

Allow yourself to feel the safety and security of the room you are sitting in now, where a safe and supportive container has been established for you to have a rich and rewarding inner experience related to your Genius qualities.

Feel your chair supporting your body, the floor of the building supporting your chair, and the very earth supporting the building you are in. This is the perfect place to be, and everything is set up to support and enhance your personal experience.

Imagine that you are walking through a wilderness, but you have no bearings. You are aware of needing to go somewhere, but you have no way of knowing where your destination is, or how to orient yourself in its direction.

Next, you meet a turtle who is walking beside a small stream. This turtle is your Genius guide. He tells you that he has found his stream and that all he needs to do is to follow it to be on his individual path. He tells you that you have a stream to follow too. And that you need to find your own stream and path.

Your Genius guide tells you that instead of wandering around looking for your stream, to sit still and listen for the sound of it. If you are quiet enough, you'll be able to hear it and find its source.

You sit quietly and close your eyes to listen for your stream.

After a while you perceive two things. One is that you hear a faint sound, off in a certain direction, of something trickling. The second is that the sound makes you feel something in particular.

What does this faint sound feel like when you hear it?

_____

_____

_____

_____

_____

_____

_____

_____

You get up and begin to move towards the sound of your stream. As you get closer and closer to it, the feeling you have becomes stronger and stronger. The more you focus on the sound, the more you feel this feeling; and the stronger the feeling gets, the clearer and louder the sound becomes.

You finally come to a spring that is bubbling happily out of the side of a hill and flowing downward. Above the spring is a large stone with your name engraved in it. Intuitively, you know that this is the exact place where your life flow has been expressed by existence as *you*.

Take a moment to be at this source of where your individuality was started by Creation.

Under your name is a word or sentence engraved that is descriptive of your connected self. What is that word or sentence?

_____

_____

_____

_____

Now look at the stream that is flowing down the hill from the spring that was created as your life flow. See that it has a direction, and a purpose to its movement and energy, that comes from the source at the spring. This is your life direction and purpose that comes from existence. You see that you can choose to be in this flow and to follow your own stream, or you can choose not to follow it.

You realize that from your vantage point at the source, you can look down this stream as if you're looking down through time at your own life experience. You can see the times where you were either walking alongside the stream or had become lost from the stream altogether.

Notice the different life experiences you've had, and how being connected or disconnected from this stream or flow has affected those life experiences.

Take some time to see if there are any differences between the experiences you've had while flowing within your own connected life stream as opposed to when you were disconnected from it.

What differences, if any, are you aware of?

_____

_____

_____

_____

_____

_____

Realize that you have an every-moment choice: to be connected to the flow of your own Genius expression that has been expressed by existence as you, or to live in a disconnected way.

With this experience solidly rooted in your present life, when you are ready, allow yourself to slowly bring your awareness back to your physical body, sitting in your chair in this room, and slowly open your eyes and be present.

INSIGHT PROTOCOL

Follow the steps below to use the Genius Way Insight Protocol to curate your experience of being a connected individual.

IDENTIFY YOUR INSIGHT

From your guided visualization experience, name an insight that occurred to you regarding your connected individualism. Think about something that you understood about yourself in a new way or from a different perspective than your usual one.

_____

_____

_____

_____

_____

_____

_____

_____

FIND YOUR INSIGHT IMAGE

Thinking about your insight, allow an image that represents your insight to come into focus in your mind's eye. What is the image that appears and represents this insight?

_____

_____

_____

_____

_____

_____

_____

_____

FIND THE SEED FEELING IN YOUR IMAGE

Holding the image of your insight in your mind's eye, allow a feeling to arise in your awareness concerning this image. What does this image make you feel? This is the seed feeling contained within your image.

_____

_____

_____

_____

_____

_____

_____

_____

COMMIT TO EXPRESSING SOMETHING FROM THE SEED FEELING

What do you want to express from your Genius as a response to your seed feeling? Identify something that you can express from your Genius insight and commit to taking an action.

I make a commitment to express my Genius self to:

_____

_____

_____

_____

_____

_____

_____

_____

MAKE A SYMBOLIC EXPRESSION

Take a small symbolic action from your insight _right now_ to start your momentum. What symbolic action do you make to acknowledge and represent your insight, image, seed feeling, and your commitment to expressing your Genius outwardly in the world?

_____

_____

_____

_____

_____

_____

_____

EXPRESS YOUR DOUBTS

Use this section to identify any doubts that are arising about your Genius process, or your ability to express from your Genius. When we can identify our doubts, we can examine them for clarity and truthfulness.

_____

_____

LIFE SKILL SEVEN AFFIRMATION

I am deeply connected to existence at a foundational level. Although I have my own thoughts, goals, and dreams, they are supported and encouraged by my connection to the creative universe. As I move through my days, I rely on this connection for feelings of safety and security. As my precious life unfolds, I rely on this connection for wisdom, strength, and guidance to make choices that bring me purpose and fulfillment.

LIFE SKILL EIGHT —
How to Connect to Your Pre-Wounded Self

CHECK IN

The previous chapter outlined the difference between our connected and disconnected selves. Using your new awareness of this quality, you can take your experience deeper by accessing your Pre-Wounded Self. In this chapter, as an additional path of identity and self-expression, you'll learn to open up a connection to the version of your life that has never been wounded.

You can see why unconditional positive self-regard is important here. It provides the pre-wounded thread of your life enough inner space to exist and begin to grow again.

CLIENT STORY

Adam was a yoga teacher in his early forties who came to me seeking help with anxiety and compulsive behavior regarding his work habits. He had been "parentified" as a child, forced to assume adult responsibilities far too early for his age, due to the neglect and irresponsibility of his alcoholic parents. It became increasingly clear to me that Adam's primary idea of himself was currently identified with the thread of his life that began during his childhood wounding, and that he was missing the connection to his pre-wounded self and his Genius.

His work compulsion was a carry-over from his traumatic childhood, where he had taken on the role in his family system to step in and take charge when situations felt out of control to him. And even though as an adult he had created a successful and stable business, marriage, and nuclear family, his actions and self-expression were largely fueled by his Wound Drive. Consequently, he wasn't able to enjoy his successes or accomplishments because his primary unconscious focus was to heal his wounds by managing chaos, and not about creating something new that he was able to comfortably enjoy.

We identified the short pre-wounded period of Adam's life as a time that was free of responsibility. What Adam needed to allow this pre-wounded self an avenue of expression was the "luxury" of not having to produce, achieve, fix, or caretake anyone or anything. Together, we developed a specific "time of enjoyment" for Adam that allowed him to take the time to reconnect to his pre-wounded child identity and give that thread of his life a healthy avenue of expression. During this "enjoyment" time, he gave himself exclusively to self-care, rest, play, and spontaneous creativity. He danced, sang, meditated, took walks, and watched movies. He made time to be silly and playful. Anything that didn't involve striving and achieving. Over time, this practice led to Adam being able to feel and access his Genius through this pre-wounded resource of himself. He discovered and was able to own his Genius qualities of holding a vision and then manifesting it, and of imparting insight to others. Picking up the pre-wounded thread of his life allowed him to step into his adult life with his Genius qualities intact and to use them in his work and life expression.

NEW LEARNING: CONNECT WITH YOUR PRE-WOUNDED SELF

Before we are all inevitably wounded in some way during our childhood, our Genius is more readily available to us, and our identities are closer and more aligned to the existential impulse and expression contained within them. To acknowledge that aspect of our identity as a *practice* is a way of reconnecting to the energy, intention, and life direction that it contains.

We can think of this pre-wounded self as the original thread of our life expression. By the time we experience our childhood woundings and internalize our first round of childhood developmental tasks, we create an additional thread or life expression and begin to follow it, forgetting that we had already possessed a primary thread based on the contents of the seed of our original life expression, given to us by existence.

What most of us don't realize is that the original life expression thread is still there, waiting to be picked up again to continue its expression, along with all of the energy, interest, and enthusiasm that it once fed us with. Remember that we do have a wounded self, and we need to continue to work with it as it appears throughout our life experiences. But also having access to our pre-wounded identity allows us to see and work with our wounds in a different context. It provides us with a level of objectivity that is impossible to have without embodying the very real part of us that isn't wounded.

Before we are wounded we are already moving in the direction of our Genius, as we are already in motion with the momentum of existence's expression of us. In other words, the child we were was on its way to grow up as a healthy and more developed expression of the original existential expression. Most of us have forgotten, however, that originally, before we were conditioned by our experiences, we were already something and someone with momentum and trajectory given by existence. This can explain why so many of us live our lives in such a state of confusion about who we are and what our life direction should be. Connecting to the pre-wounded self regularly and allowing it ample space to continue to grow again is another way of reconnecting to our Genius and of following the path of the original universal expression of who we are individually.

GUIDED EXERCISE

(Listen to the audio version on www.thegeniusway.com/guidedexercises, or read one sentence at a time, then close your eyes and follow the visuals that arise.)

Allow yourself to feel the safety and security of the room you are sitting in now, where a safe and supportive container has been established for you to have a rich and rewarding inner experience related to your Genius qualities.

Feel your chair supporting your body, the floor of the building supporting your chair, and the very earth supporting the building you are in. This is the perfect place to be, and everything is set up to support and enhance your personal experience.

Allow yourself to imagine that from the time that you were born, you were guided and encouraged to simply be your authentic Genius self.

Picture your parents, guardians, siblings, and other family members living in recognition of your special talents and qualities, and creating a space for you to express and manifest them in your life.

What kind of things do you do in your daily life?

_____

_____

_____

_____

_____

_____

_____

What are the creative expressions you explore as you are growing up?

_____

_____

_____

_____

_____

_____

_____

How does it feel to have everything you are curious about wanting to express and explore be supported and cherished by the people around you?

_____

_____

_____

_____

_____

_____

_____

As a result of this acceptance, love, and support, you can see a specific admirable quality developing in yourself.

What is this quality?

_____

_____

_____

_____

_____

_____

How does this quality affect the way you live your daily life?

_____

_____

_____

_____

_____

_____

See some examples of how your overall life experience is affected by this quality.

_____

_____

_____

_____

_____

_____

_____

Take a few moments to own this specific, admirable quality as the best part of yourself; then set an intention to keep it as you move about your world.

At this point you suddenly remember that you are actually doing a guided exercise about your Genius qualities, and that what you were experiencing may not have happened in your actual life history.

How does this realization affect the way you were seeing your life just moments ago?

_____

_____

_____

_____

_____

_____

_____

_____

What, if anything, is different about the way you see your life experience then
and now?

_____

_____

_____

_____

_____

_____

_____

_____

What has become of this admirable quality?

_____

_____

_____

_____

_____

_____

_____

_____

Can you locate this quality somewhere in your present life experience? Is it an active or dormant quality in you?

_____

_____

_____

_____

_____

_____

_____

If it is active, imagine one way in which it can become more active.

_____

_____

_____

_____

_____

_____

If it is dormant, imagine one way in which you can activate it.

_____

_____

_____

_____

_____

_____

Know that this quality is your Genius gift from birth, regardless of whether you have always been aware of it, or if you have suddenly realized this truth just now.

With this experience solidly rooted in your present life, when you are ready, allow yourself to slowly bring your awareness back to your physical body, sitting in your chair in this room, and slowly open your eyes and be present.

INSIGHT PROTOCOL

Follow the steps below to use the Genius Way Insight Protocol to curate your experience of connecting with your pre-wounded self.

IDENTIFY YOUR INSIGHT

From your guided visualization experience, name an insight that occurred to you about the life thread of your pre-wounded self. Think about something that you understood about yourself in a new way or from a different perspective than your usual one.

_____

_____

_____

_____

_____

_____

_____

_____

FIND YOUR INSIGHT IMAGE

Thinking about your insight, allow an image that represents your insight to come into focus in your mind's eye. What is the image that appears and represents this insight?

_____

_____

_____

_____

_____

_____

_____

_____

FIND THE SEED FEELING IN YOUR IMAGE

Holding the image of your insight in your mind's eye, allow a feeling to arise in your awareness concerning this image. What does this image make you feel? This is the seed feeling contained within your image.

_____

_____

_____

_____

_____

_____

_____

COMMIT TO EXPRESSING SOMETHING FROM THE SEED FEELING

What do you want to express from your Genius as a response to your seed feeling? Identify something that you can express from your Genius insight and commit to taking an action.

_____

_____

_____

_____

_____

_____

_____

_____

MAKE A SYMBOLIC EXPRESSION

Take a small symbolic action from your insight _right now_ to start your momentum. What symbolic action do you make to acknowledge and represent your insight, image, seed feeling, and your commitment to expressing your Genius outwardly in the world?

_____

_____

_____

_____

_____

_____

_____

EXPRESS YOUR DOUBTS

Use this section to identify any doubts that are arising about your Genius process, or your ability to express from your Genius. When we can identify our doubts, we can examine them for clarity and truthfulness.

_____

_____

_____

_____

_____

_____

_____

_____

LIFE SKILL EIGHT AFFIRMATION

I have a version of myself that has never been wounded. This version is available to me at any time to help me to continue to grow and develop my Genius qualities and expression. I am stronger and more complete when I include my pre-wounded self as one part of my overall identity.

LIFE SKILL NINE —
Free Will: How to Use It to Express Your Genius

CHECK IN

In the previous chapter you learned to connect to your pre-wounded self for an alternative life narrative to your current one. The storyline and thread of your pre-wounded self opens one doorway to your Genius and the qualities within it that you were born with. This chapter is about the role that free will plays in accessing our own Genius and about using our free will to express our Genius qualities. Reminder: Everyone's Genius expression is different but equally important, and your Genius is not there to be compared with others' gifts and qualities. Your Genius qualities are yours to discover for yourself and to express outwardly to the world. Your Genius expression only has to feel important *to you* to express.

Use your unconditional positive self-regard to access your free will in this chapter lesson. Take the time to see your free will as something you can express in the small moments that make up your day.

CLIENT STORY

Lori was in her mid-fifties and came to see me because she was experiencing problems in her current relationship. Her partner of four years was disrespectful, uncommitted, and generally unresponsive to her. When she expressed a personal need for connection, he called her needy and berated her for weakness. Lori had developed a long-standing habit of falling into a victim role in her relationships when her needs were not responded to. We identified Lori's issue as not being aware of, or not using, her free will to self-advocate, and instead, granting the power over her emotional self to others. Currently, she was deferring her opinion of herself and her sense of self-worth to her partner.

Lori was a highly creative painter and writer. Like many, she used her poetry and artwork to express the thoughts and feelings that she couldn't verbally express in her relationships. Our sessions helped Lori to see how she was already giving herself permission to express her free will by making a space for her Genius qualities in her artistic expression. I encouraged her to use this same free will in other aspects of her life, including in her primary relationship, where her Genius wasn't currently being expressed.

I gave Lori the task of journaling as an avenue to openly express her needs in her relationships. From that safe place, she could begin to actively use her free will and Genius without worrying about how others would respond to her. Giving herself permission to activate and recognize her free will in her journal, where she was already in touch with her Genius, was the key to creating life movement and growth for her. This opening allowed her to begin to use her free will when expressing herself to her partner and to reject his characterization of her as unreasonable, demanding, and flawed. Eventually, as in her writing and artwork, she was able to own the choices she was making in her relationships as an expression of her healthy, empowered Genius Drive. She began to see the others she had habitually placed in a power role from a different perspective in which she could now be an equal member of the relationship, and where her feelings and needs naturally deserved to be acknowledged and honored. Ultimately she chose to reject this abusive partner altogether and to form a more truthful, supportive relationship with someone who also sought a deep connection.

NEW LEARNING

Free will is the ability to do gladly that which I must do.

—Carl Jung

Although we are born as an impersonal expression of the universe, we are also sentient beings who develop conscious awareness and a sense of self. This personal sense of self allows us a good amount of free will. And free will is the ultimate creative power of the universe, because an expression of Creation with free will increases the variables and possibilities of that expression by orders of magnitude.

To illustrate this, imagine an artist creating a painting on a canvas, expressing a feeling and a vision. Then imagine the paint strokes themselves having the ability to self-animate and continue with the artist's vision by being able to change their tones, textures, shapes, and sizes. The artist creates the direction and momentum of their vision initially, and then the painting continues to evolve, consciously creating a further expression from the impulse contained within its original vision, material, or makeup.

Our personal expression is the continuance of the impersonal impulse that we were originally expressed as by existence. It is our contribution and homage to Creation. When we can listen to the deeper callings that have been imprinted in our being and create a passage for them to move from the inner to the outer, we honor the original expression by our acknowledgment of it, and by making space in our lives to continue to unfold the expression personally.

Acknowledging the existential gift of who we are at our inception as an expression of Creation can help us to use the individual agency or free will that we possess to continue the original expression of ourselves. When we do so, we're not reinventing ourselves or starting from scratch, but picking up from something that was already started by existence. Picking up this thread, we will have traction, purchase, and momentum already in our favor. We don't have to recreate ourselves when we return to the root of what we are as an expression of Creation. We can use our free will to continue the expression with our life.

When we finally understand that existing and expressing as genuinely ourselves is actually a mandate from the universe, or a task that we have been charged with, everything that comes into our field of experience can be seen as cooperating with us instead of fighting against us. We can feel that all of existence wants us to fully express the qualities we were born with and brings us life experiences that help us to achieve this fuller expression. We can know this by how it feels to align ourselves with what is personally present in us individually in our Genius Drives. The key is to use our free will to attune ourselves to the storehouse of qualities that exists there.

GUIDED EXERCISE

(Listen to the audio version on www.thegeniusway.com/guidedexercises, or read one sentence at a time, then close your eyes and follow the visuals that arise.)

Allow yourself to feel the safety and security of the room you are sitting in now, where a safe and supportive container has been established for you to have a rich and rewarding inner experience related to your Genius qualities.

Feel your chair supporting your body, the floor of the building supporting your chair, and the very earth supporting the building you are in. This is the perfect place to be, and everything is set up to support and enhance your personal experience.

Let's use three different scenarios in the same setting to open up a window into how you are using your free will. This exercise is designed to see what action you take in these given circumstances. Take note of your experience in each of these three settings.

1. See yourself walking down a city street. It is a rainy day, and you are doing your best to keep yourself as warm and dry as possible because you are about to attend an important meeting that could change your life for the better.

   As you are about to cross the street, a car runs through the crosswalk in front of you, splashing water from a puddle in the gutter all over you, soaking your clothes.

   Now you are wet and cold. What do you do now?

   _____

   _____

   _____

_____

_____

_____

_____

2. You are walking down a city street. It is early in the morning, and you have the street to yourself. You are enjoying the quiet and solitude and are feeling centered and peaceful.

    As you turn a corner, you stumble over something on the sidewalk. As you look down, you notice that you've stumbled over a thick stack of hundred-dollar bills.

    What do you do in this situation?

_____

_____

_____

_____

_____

_____

3. You are walking down a city street. It is getting dark and you are on your way home, in no particular hurry. You've had a busy day and are looking forward to getting back to your place and relaxing for the night.

    As you walk past a restaurant with tables that can be seen through its windows, you notice that an ex-lover you haven't seen for a long while is sitting alone at a table inside.

    A mix of emotions washes over you as you see this person again.

    What do you do in this situation?

_____

_____

_____

_____

_____

_____

_____

Each of these scenarios likely produced an emotional response in you, as well as an action that you chose to take. Your free will is always revealed in your actions, even while having emotional responses to your life situations. Since your Genius is revealed by your outward expression of it, your free will is the key in choosing your Genius as the basis of your expressive identity.

With this experience solidly rooted in your present life, when you are ready, allow yourself to slowly bring your awareness back to your physical body, sitting in your chair in this room, and slowly open your eyes and be present.

INSIGHT PROTOCOL

Follow the steps below to use the Genius Way Insight Protocol to curate your experience of how you are using your free will.

IDENTIFY YOUR INSIGHT

From your guided visualization experience, name an insight that occurred to you about how you used your free will. Think about something that you understood about yourself in a new way or from a different perspective than your usual one.

_____

_____

_____

_____

_____

_____

_____

FIND YOUR INSIGHT IMAGE

Thinking about your insight, allow an image that represents your insight to come into focus in your mind's eye. What is the image that appears and represents this insight?

_____

_____

_____

_____

_____

_____

_____

_____

FIND THE SEED FEELING IN YOUR IMAGE

Holding the image of your insight in your mind's eye, allow a feeling to arise in your awareness concerning this image. What does this image make you feel? This is the seed feeling contained within your image.

_____

_____

_____

_____

_____

_____

_____

COMMIT TO EXPRESSING SOMETHING FROM THE SEED FEELING

What do you want to express from your Genius as a response to your seed feeling? Identify something that you can express from your Genius insight and commit to taking an action.

I make a commitment to express my Genius self to:

_____

_____

_____

_____

_____

_____

_____

_____

MAKE A SYMBOLIC EXPRESSION

Take a small symbolic action from your insight *right now* to start your momentum. What symbolic action do you make to acknowledge and represent your insight, image, seed feeling, and your commitment to expressing your Genius outwardly in the world?

_____

_____

_____

_____

_____

_____

_____

_____

EXPRESS YOUR DOUBTS

Use this opportunity to identify any doubts that are arising about your Genius process, or your ability to express from your Genius. When we can identify our doubts, we can examine them for clarity and truthfulness.

_____

_____

_____

_____

_____

_____

_____

_____

LIFE SKILL NINE AFFIRMATION

I have the free will to choose what is most important in my life. I can choose how to respond to my present-moment experiences by acknowledging my Genius self and the creative life-direction contained in my Genius Drive. Without denying my emotions, I am free to choose my Genius Drive as the source of my actions.

LIFE SKILL TEN —
How to Identify with and Rely on
Your Genius Qualities

CHECK IN

In the previous chapter you learned about the role that free will plays in expressing your Genius. Now let's go a bit deeper into your personal Genius awareness. This chapter is about identifying some of your Genius qualities and owning and identifying with them in your daily life.

Remember that to identify with your Genius qualities as a very real part of yourself will take unconditional positive self-regard. Allow enough inner space for them to take root in your moment-to moment identity.

CLIENT STORY

Joshua was an energetic and creative man in his mid-forties who was experiencing relationship issues with his partner. He had a habit of doing all of the emotional "heavy lifting" in his prior relationships and was only mildly aware of his codependent habits in his interactions. In short, he was basing much of his self-worth on how well or how poorly his current relationship was doing.

Joshua was a "people person" who came to life while connecting with others. He felt invigorated and energized at public events and was well liked by most of his friends and acquaintances. He felt he was at his best when using his outward-facing persona. His partner often became jealous of this quality and complained that it was taking attention away from her. This left Joshua feeling guilty about expressing himself in a way that was natural to him. I could see Joshua's Genius qualities around communication and connection would be undervalued and under-expressed as long as he continued to base the value and worthiness of his identity upon his partner's responsiveness to him.

As Joshua worked to uncover his Genius qualities and identify the expressions that enlivened and energized him, he discovered how central his experiences of human connection, communication, and community were to his maintaining a healthy sense of self. We were able to map out his some of his Genius qualities regarding communication, and to develop a plan to give them an avenue of expression in his life. He began to use his natural communication and self-presentation skills to apply for interesting jobs, as well as moving his personal creative projects from the idea phase into outward expression. This exploration also led to Joshua being able to own his extroverted nature as a basic and essential aspect of himself that others, including his partner, would need to accept (or not) about him. Stepping into his life from this perspective allowed him to access his Genius Drive as a source of inspiration and energy.

NEW LEARNING

To be clear, no one is ever going to walk up to you and say with scientific certainty: "You are definitely expressing your Genius qualities right now." You will never sit before a panel of judges that will unanimously agree that you are in fact living your purpose. This being the case, the task of knowing if you are living a Genius-based life is yours and yours alone. It's up to you to define what feels fulfilling and purposeful in your own life. And for that, you will need to be able to focus on your feeling self.

Having worked with many clients and students directly on this issue over time, I've identified some general markers that indicate times and circumstances when a person is connecting to or expressing their Genius. These Genius markers are the feelings that commonly appear when individuals are engaged with self-expressive actions and activities that are core aspects of their Genius.

When you are expressing yourself in your life in the various ways that you do, in work, play, or social settings, check to see if any of the following feelings or aspects are present. This will help you develop insight into whether or not you are in your Genius self-expression. Take note of which actions you are engaging in when you feel any of these feelings:

- A sense of harmony from your thoughts and actions lining up

- A feeling of newness and deep familiarity at the same time

- An ability to "witness" creative thoughts, ideas, and expressions as they are emanating from yourself, with a sense of surprise and awe

- A sense of personal importance of what you're expressing that is difficult to explain

- A sense of satisfaction in what you're expressing; like hitting the mark, or scratching an itch

- A sense of timelessness while expressing yourself

- A sense of clarity, urgency, and authority about a thing or a subject that you recognize is important to you

- A feeling of familiarity and excitement/closeness to a thing or subject

- Renewed energy and enthusiasm

- A feeling of importance about expressing something specific

- A feeling or a sense of yourself in the future, where your life would be complete and full if you were doing or expressing this thing

- A subject or activity where you "come alive" compared to the other moments of your life

- A feeling of longing or pining for yourself as a person who expresses this or these things regularly

- A sense of "losing yourself" in an activity or subject, only to find a new and more expanded sense of self

The reason these feelings appear when you express yourself in certain ways is that they are acknowledgments of a deeper part of your identity that has existed since you were born, namely your Genius self. They can never be lost to you, even through the woundings of your life experiences. They are your in-built guide and compass to the things that are important for you in particular to create and express. Listening to these callings and aligning yourself with their inherent expressive energy makes the difference in creating a fulfilling and meaningful life.

When you practice the following guided visualization, you'll be able to identify one of your Genius qualities, experiment with it outwardly, and come to rely on its sturdiness as a part of your life expression. Remember, the Genius Way is about identifying with your Genius as a part of your everyday identity. This means that your inborn skills, interests, and talents are given credence, importance, time, and space to exist and be expressed.

GUIDED EXERCISE

(Listen to the audio version on www.thegeniusway.com/guidedexercises, or read one sentence at a time, then close your eyes and follow the visuals that arise.)

Allow yourself to feel the safety and security of the room you are sitting in now, where a safe and supportive container has been established for you to have a rich and rewarding inner experience related to your Genius qualities.

Feel your chair supporting your body, the floor of the building supporting your chair, and the very earth supporting the building you are in. This is the perfect place to be, and everything is set up to support and enhance your personal experience.

You are walking across a long, grassy lawn towards a large stone building with seven stairs leading up to the entry doors. Take a moment to look at your surroundings.

What does the building look like?

_____

_____

_____

Are there other people around?

_____

_____

What time of day or night is it?

_____

_____

As you walk up the seven stairs, you notice that the word Genius is engraved into a stone panel above the entry doors. You slowly reach for the door handle, pull the door open, and walk inside.

As you explore the interior of the building, you can see a long hallway lined with doors on each side. Each door has a person's name on it, and you realize that you are walking past individual studios where people are exploring and experimenting with their genius qualities.

You feel called to stop in front of one door and discover that this door has your name on it.

You open the door and walk inside.

What do you see?

_____

_____

_____

_____

_____

_____

Realize that everything you need to discover and explore your Genius spirit was placed in this room for you a long time ago. Someone has been keeping this room safe and clean for you since the day you were born.

On the far wall is a portrait of you as your Genius self. Your image in the painting is standing in a certain pose or position. Take note of this pose, of what you are wearing, and of the look on your face.

Underneath the portrait is a plaque, which has been engraved with something you have said as your Genius self. What does the engraving say?

_____

_____

_____

_____

As you look around the room, you see many things that are in this room because they are conducive to the expression of your particular Genius qualities.

Take a moment to discover what these things are.

As you survey all of the items in the room, you realize that you are allowed to take one of these things with you today when you leave the room.

This item is the very thing that you need *right now* in your present life to bring out one of your Genius qualities.

Which item are you drawn to?

_____

_____

_____

_____

What are you feeling as you choose this item to take with you?

_____

_____

_____

As you open the door of your Genius studio and walk out into the hall, you discover that the hall is lined with people who begin to applaud in acknowledgment as you slowly walk down the hall and out the front doors, down the steps, and across the lawn.

How does it feel to be recognized and acknowledged while you are carrying one of your Genius qualities?

_____

_____

_____

_____

_____

_____

With this experience solidly rooted in your present life, when you are ready, allow yourself to slowly bring your awareness back to your physical body, and slowly open your eyes and be present.

INSIGHT PROTOCOL

Follow the steps below to use the Genius Way Insight Protocol to curate your experience of identifying one of your Genius qualities.

IDENTIFY YOUR INSIGHT

From your guided visualization experience, name an insight that occurred to you about what one of your Genius qualities is. Think about something that you understood about yourself in a new way or from a different perspective than your usual one.

_____

_____

_____

_____

_____

_____

_____

_____

FIND YOUR INSIGHT IMAGE

Thinking about your insight, allow an image that represents your insight to come into focus in your mind's eye. What is the image that appears and represents this insight?

_____

_____

_____

_____

_____

_____

_____

_____

FIND THE SEED FEELING IN YOUR IMAGE

Holding the image of your insight in your mind's eye, allow a feeling to arise in your awareness concerning this image. What does this image make you feel? This is the seed feeling contained within your image.

_____

_____

_____

_____

_____

_____

_____

COMMIT TO EXPRESSING SOMETHING FROM THE SEED FEELING

What do you want to express from your Genius as a response to your seed feeling? Identify something that you can express from your Genius insight and commit to taking an action.

I make a commitment to express my Genius self to:

_____

_____

_____

_____

_____

_____

_____

_____

MAKE A SYMBOLIC EXPRESSION

Take a small symbolic action from your insight *right now* to start your momentum. What symbolic action do you make to acknowledge and represent your insight, image, seed feeling, and your commitment to expressing your Genius outwardly in the world?

_____

_____

_____

_____

_____

_____

_____

EXPRESS YOUR DOUBTS

Use this section to identify any doubts that are arising about your Genius process, or your ability to express from your Genius. When we can identify our doubts, we can examine them for clarity and truthfulness.

_____

_____

_____

_____

_____

_____

_____

_____

LIFE SKILL TEN AFFIRMATION

I acknowledge the qualities of my individual Genius self as core elements of my personal identity. As I move through my life, I refer to them for guidance and direction in making life choices and personal decisions. I already have what I need to create a meaningful life within me as the qualities of my Genius self. I trust that I am continuing the existential expression I was born with by expressing my Genius.

PERSONAL CONTENT SECTION

NOW IT'S TIME TO gather the experiential information you've uncovered in the Life Skill chapters in one place.

To see a more complete picture of your Genius, we're going to bring together your primaconscious content that was uncovered in the ten Life Skill chapters. Using this method of collection, you will distill your own experience into a very concentrated image of your Genius identity. This clear and powerful image of your Genius self will be your guide and focus moving forward in your life. You'll be able to refer to this image of your Genius as you make your life decisions large and small.

Go back to the Insight Protocol in Life Skill chapters one through ten and read what you wrote down from your inner experiences. As you review the sections—Insights, Images, Seed Feelings, Commitments, and Symbolic Expressions—circle or highlight the words or sentences that feel most true and compelling to you. Choosing the words or sentences that feel most important is part of the process of becoming clear and focused about what your Genius qualities are. Copy the circled words and sentences from each part of the Insight Protocol here, in the space provided. It doesn't matter if there are duplicate words or sentences; just work through your material in each chapter and write it down.

INSIGHTS

Write the circled words/phrases of your insights from the Life Skill chapters one through ten here.

Chapter 1

_____

_____

_____

Chapter 2

_____

_____

_____

Chapter 3

_____

_____

_____

Chapter 4

_____

_____

_____

Chapter 5

_____

_____

_____

Chapter 6

_____

_____

_____

Chapter 7

_____

_____

_____

Chapter 8

_____

_____

_____

Chapter 9

_____

_____

_____

Chapter 10

_____

_____

_____

IMAGES

Write the circled words of your images from your insights from the Life Skill chapters one through ten here.

Chapter 1

_____

_____

_____

Chapter 2

_____

_____

_____

Chapter 3

_____

_____

_____

Chapter 4

_____

_____

_____

Chapter 5

_____

_____

_____

Chapter 6

_____

_____

_____

Chapter 7

_____

_____

_____

Chapter 8

_____

_____

_____

Chapter 9

_____

_____

_____

Chapter 10

_____

_____

_____

SEED FEELINGS

Write the circled words of your Seed Feelings from your images from the Life Skill chapters one through ten here.

Chapter 1

_____

_____

_____

Chapter 2

_____

_____

_____

Chapter 3

_____

_____

_____

Chapter 4

_____

_____

_____

Chapter 5

_____

_____

_____

Chapter 6

_____

_____

_____

Chapter 7

_____

_____

_____

Chapter 8

_____

_____

_____

Chapter 9

_____

_____

_____

Chapter 10

_____

_____

_____

COMMITMENTS

Write the circled words of your commitments to expressing from your seed feelings from the Life Skill chapters one through ten here.

Chapter 1

_____

_____

_____

Chapter 2

_____

_____

_____

Chapter 3

_____

_____

_____

Chapter 4

_____

_____

_____

Chapter 5

_____

_____

_____

Chapter 6

_____

_____

_____

Chapter 7

_____

_____

_____

Chapter 8

_____

_____

_____

Chapter 9

_____

_____

_____

Chapter 10

_____

_____

_____

SYMBOLIC EXPRESSIONS

Write the circled words of your symbolic expressions from the Life Skill chapters one through ten here.

Chapter 1

_____

_____

_____

Chapter 2

_____

_____

_____

Chapter 3

_____

_____

_____

Chapter 4

_____

_____

_____

Chapter 5

_____

_____

_____

Chapter 6

_____

_____

_____

Chapter 7

_____

_____

_____

Chapter 8

_____

_____

_____

Chapter 9

_____

_____

_____

Chapter 10

_____

_____

_____

Great. Now that you've distilled your primaconscious material into a more focused format, let's go through each of these five sections and notice if there are any insights, images, seed feelings, commitments, or symbolic expressions that repeat or appear as recurrent themes. The theme or themes that appear from your inner work are showing you the direction in which your primaconscious and Genius Drive are naturally moving. Circle them and rewrite them as words, phrases, or sentences here.

INSIGHTS

_____

_____

_____

IMAGES

_____

_____

_____

SEED FEELINGS

_____

_____

_____

COMMITMENTS

_____

_____

_____

SYMBOLIC EXPRESSIONS

_____

_____

_____

Are you beginning to see a clearer picture of your Genius? Getting down to the basic elements of your Genius qualities paints the picture of what is in your primaconscious and Genius Drive to express outwardly in the world.

Remember that there is an inherent energy and momentum supporting the expression of your Genius, because existence itself is what initially expressed these qualities in you in potential within your Genius DNA.

CONCLUSION

YOU HAVE JUST COMPLETED a process that has furnished you with information, answers, and truths about your inner Genius self.

You also have ten essential life skills to practice and develop throughout the rest of your lifetime.

You have distilled the primaconscious material that you brought into your conscious awareness into a few concentrated sentences that describe your Genius qualities and Genius Drive. These essential sentences describing your Genius actually hold the experiential energy of the journey you took to bring them from your primaconscious to your conscious self. They represent the fuel of your Genius Drive and have come from your deep existential inheritance.

Now be sure to use them. Respect and enjoy them.

They are vitally important to how you show up in your life as your Genius self. Create avenues of expression for them. Use the potency they contain as guidance and direction as you move forward.

Remember to use the three Genius Way principles of *Insight*, *Commitment*, and *Practice* to integrate what you have uncovered into your life experience and identity. Using these three principles allows you to own what you have learned about your Genius self. You can step into this ownership by outwardly expressing what you have found.

I'm going to share one more lesson from the Genius Way process with you.

One of the exercises I teach in my Genius Way workshops is to show my students various Rorschach inkblots and have them describe what they see. These inkblot images are "projective" exercises, in that they have absolutely no meaning besides what the observer projects onto them from their own psychological material. The observer therefore is always seeing and describing something about themself rather than about the image. After the participants describe what they see in the random shapes of the inkblots, I hand each one of them a handheld mirror and ask them again to describe what they see as they look at their own reflected image. I can say that nearly without exception, the psychological projections onto each person's mirrored image are overwhelmingly negative, critical, and judgmental.

For the final lesson of this book, instead of a mirror, I'll ask you to get or take a picture of yourself, as you are today. It doesn't have to be a glamorous shot with professional lighting or your most flattering angle. Just a photo of yourself as you are right now.

Look at that picture and acknowledge the first thing that you see and feel.

If you find yourself judging or criticizing, you can see one of the issues that the Genius Way is designed to address.

Instead, and as an ongoing practice, use the quality of *unconditional positive self-regard* that you've developed throughout the Genius Way process. Look at this picture at least once a day to remind you of your Genius self. If judgments and criticisms appear, simply acknowledge them and then allow them to fade away. Make the effort to see *this* picture of yourself as the creative spark that was expressed by existence, before you had ever learned to judge or criticize yourself, and as the person who was valuable enough to be imbued with these particular gifts and talents. See this image of yourself more deeply and compassionately, as if you are viewing a picture of a loved one, overlooking any flaws or inconsistencies, seeing all the way through to the intrinsic worth and value you contain. Within this original expression are your existence-given Genius qualities and callings that beckon you to live your meaningful and fulfilling life.

The fuller manifestation of your particular Genius seed belongs out in the world. Others are open and ready for your expression to inspire them to express their own Genius.

Remember George Bernard Shaw's quote about the acorn exploding into an oak?

I have one final question for you.

What will you do with the fierce energy of your own Genius Drive?

ABOUT THE AUTHOR

Ben Hummell is a Licensed Psychotherapist and author, and the creator of The Genius Way® Life Skills System.

At the age of nineteen Ben was drawn to the practice of meditation and soon dedicated himself to a life of spiritual discipline and the goal of enlightenment. He found himself developing and expressing his talent for teaching spirituality and helping to guide other spiritual seekers on their individual paths at an early age.

Ben's enthusiasm for creativity, community, and spiritual practice fueled his path from his twenties through his forties. During those thirty years, he was a spiritual counselor and teacher, public speaker, entrepreneur, and musician.

At the age of forty-nine, Ben found himself in the midst of a difficult life transition; a spiritual disillusionment and loss of faith that led him to yet another search for identity, life meaning, and purpose.

After years of disorientation, confusion, and struggle, he came to learn about the ancient Greco-Roman concept of a Genius spirit that is born with every individual—a life-guiding force complete with talents, abilities, and a genuine calling to a unique expression of one's gifts. His research into Genius helped Ben to realize that one of his Genius traits had always been to help others to navigate difficult life transitions and encourage them during that process.

Ben's clinical practice as a Depth Psychotherapist allowed him to recognize a central theme in the human condition. Besides needing to heal our psychological wounds, we have each been given an existential task to express the unique gifts contained in our Genius self.

Ben found that by helping his clients to uncover and express their innate Genius qualities, they were able to rise to meet this life task, and create forward life movement with a sense of meaning and purpose. He has seen many pivotal changes and resolutions to problems occur in people's lives when they uncover their unique Genius talents and embody them actively in the world.

If you would like to learn more about Ben Hummell's books, courses, and workshops, and keep up to date with new information about expressing your Genius, please visit: www.thegeniusway.com.

Made in the USA
Columbia, SC
15 February 2025

53881152R00102